DATE DUE

RANDOM HOUSE LAW MANUALS FROM HALT

Using a Lawyer . . .
And What to Do If Things Go Wrong
A Step-by-Step Guide

Everyday Contracts
Protecting Your Rights
A Step-by-Step Guide

If You Want to Sue a Lawyer . . .
A Directory of Legal Malpractice Attorneys

Probate
Settling an Estate
A Step-by-Step Guide

Real Estate
The Legal Side to Buying a House, Condo, or Co-op
A Step-by-Step Guide

Small Claims Court
Making Your Way Through the System
A Step-by-Step Guide

OTHER RANDOM HOUSE LAW MANUALS

Personal Bankruptcy and Debt Adjustment
A Fresh Start
A Step-by-Step Guide by Kenneth Doran

IF YOU WANT TO SUE A LAWYER . . .

A Directory of Legal Malpractice Attorneys

IF YOU WANT TO SUE A LAWYER ...

A Directory of Legal Malpractice Attorneys

KAY OSTBERG and THERESA MEEHAN RUDY

in Association with HALT

RANDOM HOUSE NEW YORK

R346.033   O85i

c./

All rights reserved under the International and Pan-American Copyright
Conventions. Published in the United States by Random House, Inc., New
York, and simultaneously in Canada by Random House of Canada Lim-
ited, Toronto.

This work was originally published in different form by HALT—An Organization of Americans for Legal Reform in 1989 as *Directory of Lawyers
Who Sue Lawyers.*

HALT—An Organization of Americans for Legal Reform is a national,
nonprofit, nonpartisan public interest group with more than 150,000
members. Located at 1319 F St. NW, Suite 300, Washington, DC 20004, its
goals are to enable people to handle their legal affairs simply, affordably
and equitably. HALT's education and advocacy programs strive to im-
prove the quality, reduce the costs and increase the accessibility of the
civil justice system. Its activities are funded by members' contributions.

The directory listing of legal malpractice attorneys was compiled by
Theresa Meehan Rudy. Substantial assistance with this book was provided by Richard Hébert, Kristine Dressel and Marci Rose.

Grateful acknowledgment is made to West Publishing Company for permission to reprint graphs from *Legal Malpractice,* 3rd edition (West Publishing Company, 1989), by Ronald E. Mallen and Jeffrey M. Smith.
Reprinted by permission.

Library of Congress Cataloging-in-Publication Data

Ostberg, Kay.
  If you want to sue a lawyer— a directory of legal malpractice
attorneys / Kay Ostberg and Theresa Meehan Rudy in association
with HALT.
  p.   cm. — (A Random House practical law manual)
  Includes bibliographical references.
  ISBN 0–679–73870–3. — $10.00
1. Lawyers—Malpractice—United States—Popular works.
2. Lawyers—United States—Directories.   I. Rudy, Theresa.
II. HALT, Inc.   III. Title.   IV. Series.
KF313.Z90865   1991
346.7303'3—dc20   91–25252
[347.30633]   CIP

Book design by Charlotte Staub

Manufactured in the United States of America

Revised Edition

This book is dedicated to George Milko,
who served as Director of Education for HALT
until his death in April 1991.
George Milko, a faithful public servant
during his lifetime, was a pioneer in
the legal reform movement.
He was also a beloved
colleague and friend
to all at HALT.

Contents

IF YOU WANT TO
SUE A LAWYER . . .
*A Directory of Legal
Malpractice Attorneys*

Introduction

Members of the legal profession traditionally have been reluctant to sue their fellow lawyers, and those willing to do so are picky about the cases they take because malpractice cases are hard to win.

However, times are changing. Insurance actuaries report that claims against lawyers are increasing by 20 percent a year. And as the number of claims rises, so does the number of lawyers who handle such cases.

> This directory lists lawyers in every state who are willing to sue other lawyers for legal malpractice. *Neither HALT nor the publisher makes any guarantees about the lawyers listed, and with few exceptions, these lawyers have no relationship with us.* We do not know how long each lawyer has been in practice, how many legal malpractice cases each has handled or whether or not clients have been satisfied with the representation they received.

For these reasons, we urge you to read and consider carefully the plain-language information the book provides. You should also become familiar with the basics of legal malpractice law to be found in Chapter 4. This information is included to help you evaluate your case and hire a lawyer you can work with and have confidence in. Read it before shopping for and hiring a malpractice lawyer. It will give you a solid foundation upon which to build your client-attorney relationship.

The chapter on shopping for a lawyer gives guidelines to help you:

- Understand the range of services and prices available
- Compare opinions of your malpractice problem
- Select a lawyer who is most likely to handle your case the way you expect

Understanding legal malpractice law helps you:

- Make an assessment of your chances of winning
- Make informed decisions as your case progresses
- Ask a lawyer knowledgeable questions

If you already have a working relationship with a lawyer, the introductory material can help you identify potential trouble spots in time to avoid or fix them.[1]

This directory also includes information on how to file a complaint (Appendix I), a state-by-state listing of bar association programs that resolve complaints against lawyers (Appendix II), a diagram of the procedural steps involved in a lawsuit (Appendix III), a list of private alternative dispute resolution (ADR) programs (Appendix IV), a glossary of basic terms used in the text or for procedures in a typical civil suit (Appendix V), an annotated bibliography of other resources on client-attorney relations, malpractice law and directories of lawyers (Appendix VI), and a form for you to use to suggest other lawyers to add to the next edition of this directory (Appendix VII).

---

[1] If you have a problem, refer to our book *Using a Lawyer . . . And What to Do If Things Go Wrong,* Kay Ostberg, Random House, 1990. It discusses strategies for solving problems, the pros and cons of firing a lawyer and how to file a formal complaint against a lawyer.

A WORD ABOUT TERMS

This directory uses common, everyday language. Where familiarity with a legal term would be helpful, the legal word or phrase is also included. The better acquainted you are with these terms, the more confidently you'll be able to hire a lawyer and manage your case.

In this text, the term "misconduct" refers to an offense that can be the basis of a lawsuit. Lawyers often use the term to describe an ethical violation of a state's rules of professional conduct. Under that definition, misconduct is not always a basis for a lawsuit.

WHY HIRE A LAWYER?

It does not make sense to sue whenever you have a legal question or problem. You do have options other than legal malpractice litigation. They are outlined in Chapter 1 of this book, and we encourage you to consider them before deciding to sue.

If you do decide to sue, your next step is to decide whether to hire a lawyer. Many legal tasks can be done using self-help materials or nonlawyer experts. Malpractice cases, however, are complex and involve an opponent who knows the legal system. You're fighting on your opposition's turf under rules written by, and all too familiar to, the opposition. Because of this, your chances of winning a legal malpractice action in court are extremely small if you represent yourself. This is one of the instances in which you'll do best if you hire a lawyer.

HOW WE COMPILED THE DIRECTORY

The names and addresses listed in this directory were collected from several sources. First, all current directories of lawyers or law firms that handle malpractice cases were checked. (These directories are listed in Appendix VI.) We then added lawyers from HALT's legal services referral network, and in states with fewer than five lawyers listed, added names from lawyer referral services in the state. All the attorneys listed either completed and returned a questionnaire confirming their interest in taking legal malpractice cases on behalf of clients or provided verbal confirmation of their interest over the telephone.

READING TIPS

You should note a few important points about the listings:

- *They are not exhaustive.* You may find other lawyers who handle legal malpractice cases by asking for referrals from the lawyers who are listed or by checking local lawyer referral services for the latest listings. (If you find a good one, let us know by sending the form on page 127.)
- *Almost none of the lawyers handles only legal malpractice cases.* Many are general practitioners, general malpractice specialists or lawyers who indicated that although they have never taken a legal malpractice case, they are willing to do so.
- *Some of those listed may also take cases defending attorneys against legal malpractice actions.*
- *Many lawyers caution* that their decision to take a case is based on how much money is at stake and whether or not they or someone else in their firm has had dealings with the lawyer a client wants to sue.
- *All business agreements* are to be worked out between you and the attorney you select.

CHAPTER 1

BEFORE
YOU SUE

If your lawyer is guilty of misconduct, you naturally want to get your money back for the damage that was caused. However, deciding whether to sue for legal malpractice is rarely that simple. In addition to assessing your case in light of the material on malpractice law in this directory, you should consider the following five factors:

Time   Chapters 3 and 4 will help you assess how complicated your legal malpractice case is. Depending on the complexity, it could take years to settle or to pursue in court. Malpractice lawyers estimate that cases take an average of two years, with some taking up to six.

Cost   To pursue a malpractice case costs money: You must pay lawyer fees and expenses. These can run extremely high, depending on the facts of your case, your negotiations when hiring your malpractice lawyer, and how the lawyer you are suing (or the malpractice insurance carrier) decides to fight the case. Make sure you know the financial, emotional and other costs of suing and balance them against a realistic assessment of what you can expect to win.

Unfortunately, it's rarely cost-effective to take a legal malpractice case to court unless you have a good chance of winning at least $25,000. Most lawyers won't take cases unless they have a good chance of winning at least $50,000. If you have a case "worth" less than $25,000, you do have some alternatives that we will discuss later in this chapter.

Energy   If you have already been burned by one lawyer, you may find it difficult to work with another. Assess your ability to take another crack at the legal system, given your past experiences. Most people have little idea of what it takes to pursue a legal claim or to work with a lawyer. Because you've been through it, you do. Keep that in mind when you decide your course of action.

If you pursue your case primarily because you're angry or want revenge, chances are that that alone won't sustain you through the years these cases can take. Consider filing a grievance complaint (see page 11) instead or writing a letter to the editor of your local newspaper.

Chances of Success   Assess your chances of success carefully. Remember, the legal system is set up primarily to compensate you with money for your losses or injury. Weigh all the financial details. Consider getting a second legal opinion as to your chances of winning as well as the amount you're likely to win. Although legal cases are never certain, lawyering is a business, and lawyers should be able to estimate this sum for you: It's what they do before *they* decide whether to take a case.

Other Options   Consider alternatives to suing. Using one of these options may resolve your dispute with the expenditure of less time, money and stress. Standard alternatives to litigation include direct negotiation, mediation, arbitration and small claims court. In the case of lawyer misconduct, they also include complaining to your state's disciplinary agency, filing a claim with a client security trust fund, or asking for arbitration of the malpractice or fee dispute.

ALTERNATIVES TO SUING

You have several alternatives to pursuing a malpractice claim in court. Choosing any of these does not cut off your right to sue for malpractice unless you sign a mediated agreement or agree to binding arbitration.

Direct Negotiation   In some instances, you may get what you want by discussing it directly with the lawyer or, possibly, the lawyer's insurance carrier. A lawyer who misses the court's filing deadline *(statute of limitations)* or steals your money may be willing to settle directly with you, particularly if that person wants to stay in business. However, be careful. If a lawyer settles directly with you, without reporting your complaint to the malpractice insurer, you could lose the right to get recovery from that insurer.

Also, be careful not to settle for too little. In fact, many states have a rule requiring a lawyer to notify you in writing that you should hire a lawyer to protect your rights. This is because lawyers are trained in negotiating settlements. Check any settlement offer with a knowledgeable professional, usually another lawyer.

Especially if you have ongoing business with a lawyer, you may want to settle your differences as amicably as possible. To do that, you'll need to talk to and correspond with the lawyer, prepare questions and be willing to listen to and answer questions about what you want and expect.

If you're trying to settle a problem directly, be sure to confirm spoken agreements and telephone conversations in a letter. It's easiest to keep things clearly understood on both sides if someone writes them down. It may also be valuable to have a written record of the course of your negotiations (see also Chapter 5).

Mediation   Mediation occurs when two or more people sit down with a neutral third person to negotiate an agreement. Mediation sessions are informal and designed to allow the mediator to help both sides agree on how to resolve a problem. To be legally enforceable as a contract, any agreement must be in writing and signed by both parties.

Not all kinds of disputes are appropriate for mediation, and so far mediators have rarely taken client-attorney disputes. The technique works best for people whose relationship will continue after the settlement is reached. It is often used by divorcing couples, disputing neighbors, or landlords and their tenants. Mediation is offered by some local courts and by private mediators (see Appendix IV). Also, check with your local courts and the telephone Yellow Pages for listings. Before you hire a mediator, be sure you find out:

- If the mediator handles lawyer-client disputes
- How much mediation costs
- Whether volunteer mediators are used
- How the mediators are trained
- How long the mediator has been in practice and whether any cases handled were similar to yours
- How long it usually takes to mediate a settlement and what the mediator's track record on settlements is
- What former clients say about the mediator

General Arbitration   In arbitration, the two sides submit written summaries of their arguments and positions to a neutral third party or a panel of up to three arbitrators.

The arbitrator or panel then holds a hearing, listens to both sides, considers the evidence presented and makes a decision. If both sides have agreed to binding arbitration, the decision will be upheld by a court.

Arbitration first became popular for resolving labor-management disputes. It has since expanded to many other fields, including client-attorney disputes, a small number of which are now resolved in arbitration. More formal than mediation but less formal than litigation, arbitration is offered by organizations such as the American Arbitration

Association and by private arbitrators (see Appendix IV). If you opt for arbitration, follow the shopping tips listed for finding a mediator.

Filing a Complaint   Every state has a lawyer-run agency that processes consumer complaints against lawyers (see Appendix II). In about one third of the states these agencies are run directly by state bar associations. Their only function is to police violations of the state's rules of professional conduct, based on a model written by the American Bar Association. This code spells out the rules lawyers must work by and is enforced by the highest court of the state.

The four types of discipline that agencies can mete out include:

- *Private reprimand* A written or oral chastising of the lawyer. It is not made public.
- *Public Reprimand* A public notice listing the lawyer's misconduct, usually published in a bar association journal.
- *Suspension* Suspending a lawyer's license to practice law in a given state for a specified time, ranging from a few days to several years.
- *Disbarment* Removing a lawyer from practicing law in a specified state for at least five years, usually with a hearing required for readmission.

The attorney discipline system is riddled with flaws. More than 90,000 complaints are filed each year with these agencies, but only about 2 percent of the complaints result in more than private reprimand. Clients often don't file complaints because the process takes too long, it takes place in secret, it limits clients' rights to present their own cases or to appeal decisions and it *does not provide any compensation.*

Nevertheless, clients who have problems with their lawyers should file complaints with these agencies if only to document those problems. Also, complaining about your attorney's misconduct may help assure that future clients are protected. You may be filing the tenth complaint against a lawyer, establishing a pattern that the agency cannot ignore.

Fee Arbitration   Some state and local bar associations have fee arbitration programs that handle complaints of lawyer overcharging or incorrect billing. The arbitration panels decide what fee is owed the lawyer. The advantages of taking a disputed fee to arbitration is that it is quick and inexpensive, and it allows you to present your case without having to hire another lawyer.

To find out more about fee arbitration in your state, contact your state bar association (Appendix II). The arbitration office will probably ask you to fill out a formal request for arbitration, including a description of your complaint. If your case is accepted, you'll get an informal hearing before a panel of arbitrators.

Fee arbitration programs do have flaws, however. A few states do not offer such programs, and only about thirty-one states and the District of Columbia offer arbitration statewide. In almost every state the attorney can refuse to submit to arbitration. Moreover, arbitration panels are not generally allowed to use either the fact of malpractice or the fact that you received incompetent service as a reason for adjusting the fee you owe. The panel has the power only to determine the agreed-upon fee and whether the work was completed, and therefore whether the fee was earned.

Client Security Trust Funds   Most states have a special fund set up to reimburse the money stolen from clients by their lawyers. To be reimbursed for money stolen or "misappropriated" by your lawyer, simply apply to your state bar's client security trust fund (Appendix II).

These programs also have limitations. Because the funds are run by state bar associations and supported by lawyers' dues, clients have no legal right to reimbursement and thus no right to appeal a denial. In addition, most state bars limit the amount that is refundable, regardless of how much was stolen. The maximum that will be refunded in any one case can range between $3,000 and $100,000, depending on the state. Finally, in recent years some states have turned down claims because the fund was underfinanced and had run out of money.

Malpractice Arbitration   The Kentucky State Bar and the District of Columbia Bar have created the nation's first legal malpractice arbitration programs. These initiatives are in response to a growing recognition that, though clients may have valid claims against lawyers, if the disputed amount is in the $5,000-to-$10,000 range, they have no place to go for a fair hearing and compensation.

It is too early to evaluate these programs. Although there is certainly a need for an effective alternative to suing for these claims, it is not yet clear that these programs will do a good job of handling client complaints.

Small Claims Court   Small claims courts were set up to allow people to bring relatively small legal claims to an efficient, inexpensive, informal setting hospitable to consumers. You do not need a lawyer to take a case to small claims court, although most states don't forbid it. The major limitations are that the maximum you can sue for ranges between $1,000 and $5,000, depending on the rules in your area, and some consumers find these courts intimidating.

If you decide to try this option, refer to our book *Small Claims Court.*[1] It provides step-by-step information on bringing a case in small claims court.

---

[1]*Small Claims Court: Making Your Way Through the System,* Theresa Meehan Rudy, Random House, 1990.

CHAPTER 2

LAWYER SHOPPING

Lawyers sell legal services. As a customer, you should choose the service you want and come to an agreement, preferably in writing, on the terms of the purchase. *You* are the employer. It's *your* money, *your* property, and *your* rights that are at stake.

Careful lawyer shopping is important; it is your first and best opportunity to make sure you are hiring a lawyer who will handle your case competently and according to your wishes. This section briefly summarizes techniques you can use to shop for and choose a lawyer, with particular attention to hiring a legal malpractice lawyer.

It's emotionally and financially difficult to hire a malpractice lawyer after having had a bad experience with another lawyer. However, you may have learned a valuable lesson from that bad experience: how to shop wisely for a lawyer and how to spot problems early and prevent them from growing.

LIST YOUR PROSPECTS

Your first step is to generate a list of prospects. This directory will provide some names to get you started. You can also ask for recommendations from business acquaintances, relatives, friends and professionals, such as clergy, social workers and physicians. Solicit lawyers' names from people whose judgment you consider sound. You can also get names from lawyer referral services in your area.

It may take time to round up prospects. In some areas of the country you may find it all but impossible to find a lawyer to take your case against another lawyer.

When you generate your list of lawyers, you may need to choose someone who practices outside the town or county in which the lawyer you want to sue works. You'll need to do this because many lawyers, particularly in rural areas, will not sue another lawyer who works in the same town, who is probably a member of the same local bar association or whom they see frequently in court.

When you have compiled a list of prospects, your search has just begun. Use the list the way you would use a page of want ads for used cars. Contact the prospects you've identified and assess the quality of the services they offer.

INITIAL CONTACT

Telephone each prospect. This initial contact will help you shorten your list. Prepare for the calls by writing down the questions you want to ask each lawyer. If you are well organized, you will save both yourself and the attorney time and demonstrate your intention to remain in charge of your legal affairs in a businesslike, professional way. At this point, remember that you are calling lawyers to find out about their experience and capabilities, not to explain all the details of your case.

Use your telephone call to:

1. *Identify yourself and explain* that you are looking for a lawyer to sue another lawyer for malpractice.
2. *Determine whether the lawyer charges* for an in-person initial consultation. What is the cost?

3. *Ask questions* you think are important and that can be answered briefly. For example:
   - Are you the lawyer who would handle my case? If not, may I speak to that lawyer?
   - How long have you been in practice?
   - Have you handled a legal malpractice case before?
   - How many such cases have you handled and with what outcome?
   - What are your usual rates for legal malpractice cases?
   - Are your fees negotiable?
   - Can you refer me to clients for whom you have handled legal malpractice cases? Other types of cases?
   - Do you have a standard written agreement I could review in advance? If not, do you typically sign written agreements with clients?
   - Do you carry malpractice insurance? What are the terms of your insurance policy?
4. *Answer questions* the attorney may have.
5. *Schedule an in-person interview* if the prospect still appears worth pursuing.

You can discover a lot from this telephone call. If, for example, you are not allowed to talk with the lawyer who will be working on your case, this tells you something about how the office is run. The senior attorney may be the "salesperson" prepared for your questions. The junior attorney who will handle your case may be less experienced.

Keep in mind that although legal malpractice suits are more common than in the past, few lawyers are legal malpractice experts. In many ways this is a new and expanding field of law.

Expect to be asked the name of the lawyer you want to sue. Lawyers ask this to screen out cases against lawyers they don't want to or can't sue because of a conflict of interest, as well as out of idle curiosity. If you feel comfortable giving the name of the attorney, do so, but first extract a promise that the lawyer will not reveal the information and that the name will be considered a client confidence.

THE INTERVIEW

The initial visit to the lawyer's office allows you to find out as much as you can about the lawyer. This is not the time to tell the attorney everything there is to know about your malpractice claim. However, you do want to give a brief summary of your case so the lawyer can accurately explain how it should be handled. You have four goals in this interview:

1. *Determine whether the lawyer is experienced and willing* to undertake your case.

2. *Understand what services will be performed* for you and how much you will be charged for them.

3. *Learn whether you will be comfortable* working with the lawyer.

4. *Hear the lawyer's initial assessment* of your chances of winning and what you can recover.

Prepare for the interview by writing a brief summary of your case, including all relevant dates and all major facts. The lawyer will need some of this information immediately, and you can save time if you're ready with it. Also prepare a list of questions to ask.

During the interview, make notes of the lawyer's answers so you can compare them with what other lawyers say before you make your final choice. One warning: don't be so preoccupied with your "script" of questions that you forget to listen to the answers for both content and style. Be businesslike, listen carefully and communicate accurately and concisely.

FEE ARRANGEMENTS

A client-attorney employment agreement is a legally binding contract that's enforceable in court. It spells out the terms of your relationship with the lawyer, the work that will be done and the fees you can be charged. You should have a written agreement with any attorney you hire. If you don't, you'll have no way of proving what you agreed to. It will be your word against your lawyer's.

During the interview, discuss possible fee arrangements and what would be covered in the employment agreement. If you don't have an agreement that says otherwise, the law allows your lawyer to collect a "reasonable" fee—and the definition of "reasonable" varies from state to state. Some courts have even considered fees as high as 60 percent of the award to be "reasonable." This is why it is so critical that you negotiate your fee and get it *in writing* and *in advance.*

Discuss the following points with prospective lawyers and put your decisions about them into your agreement with the person you hire.

Fees Most malpractice lawyers charge a *contingency fee.* Under a contingency fee system, if you win, your lawyer gets a percentage of the winnings; if you lose, the lawyer doesn't get any fee. Typical percentages for legal malpractice cases range from 25 to 50 percent. The theory behind the contingency fee is simple: The attorney assumes a risk of losing; the greater the risk, the bigger the percentage.

The problem with this method is that the fee is not based on the amount of time and work done on the case. No matter how many hours the lawyer puts into the case, if you win, the lawyer gets a preset percentage of the award. If you calculate what the lawyer is paid for each hour of work, a contingency fee often works out to be a windfall for the lawyer when compared with typical hourly rates.

If you agree to pay a contingency fee, be sure to specify that the percentage be calculated *after* expenses have been subtracted from the award. This can result in substantial savings.

Some lawyers offer a sliding scale, with the percentage increasing at each stage of the case. For example, the lawyer may collect 35 percent if you settle before trial, 45 percent if you go to trial, and 50 percent if the case goes to an appellate court.

Although a sliding scale might seem attractive at first glance, be wary. If you agree to it, your lawyer may try to get you to accept settlement because going to trial involves more time, work and risk of losing. In some instances, a lawyer may press you to settle when you would do better financially to continue pursuing the case. Also recognize that when you weigh a settlement offer you'll have to pay an additional 10 percent in attorney fees if you reject it and go to trial.

Those who defend the contingency fee system argue that lawyers deserve a windfall because of the risk of losing the case and getting no fee. They also believe the fee is warranted because clients don't have to pay up front. In fact, however, lawyers rarely take chancy cases, and just because clients pay later doesn't mean they should have to pay an unreasonably high fee. Moreover, the contingency fee structure potentially pits you against your attorney—not a healthy relationship.

You may find a lawyer willing to take your case at an hourly rate. If your lawyer charges $150 an hour, your fee will be $150 multiplied by the number of hours—or partial hours—worked. This fee is charged whether you win or lose, and whether you go to trial or not.

Using an hourly rate can work to your financial advantage if you win the case. Review the figures your lawyer has estimated. Look at the amount the lawyer believes you will win and how many hours of work it is estimated it will take to complete the case. Compare the hourly rate to the probable contingency fee divided by the hours of work involved.

Expenses   In addition to lawyers' fees, whether you win or lose, you'll have to pay any costs associated with handling your case. These will probably include court filing fees plus fees for expert witnesses, transcripts, stenographers, photocopying, mailing and, especially if you hire an out-of-town attorney, long-distance telephone calls and transportation. If your case goes to trial, these expenses can be quite high.

Ask your prospective lawyer to estimate the costs and tell you when they'll have to be paid. You may be asked to give a deposit *(retainer)* to cover initial expenses. This can vary from $1,000 to $10,000. Set a cap on the total expenses you can be billed for. If more expense money is needed, make sure your agreement requires your lawyer to get your written approval. Also write into the contract that your lawyer must get your approval for any major expenses above a specified amount, such as $500.

Expert witnesses are particularly expensive, but you will need one or more if your case goes to trial. Fees range from $1,000 to more than $3,000 per expert, per day, and you will have to pay not only for the time spent testifying at trial, but also for trial preparation, including document review and research, pretrial questioning, travel and waiting at the courthouse.

Billing Arrangements   How and when you'll be billed should also be spelled out in your agreement. Bills not only provide a history of your dealings with your lawyer, they are also a useful management tool because they remind the lawyer to send you periodic progress reports on your case.

Ask for monthly itemized bills, particularly if you are being charged by the hour. If you anticipate long periods of inaction on your case, you can modify this requirement. Make sure that all work will be itemized and that support staff hours will be listed separately from attorney hours. Support staff billing rates should be lower than attorneys' rates.

If you have agreed to an hourly rate, check your bills carefully when they arrive to be sure you aren't being charged more lawyer time than necessary to complete tasks (over-lawyering) or billed for work never done (bill padding).

Timetable Your agreement should estimate the total time the case will take and spell out as precisely as possible the tasks the lawyer will perform and how long those tasks will take. The lawyer may find the time difficult to predict, but even "ballpark" estimates are extremely valuable. This timetable will allow you to judge the progress of your case, and it should identify the logical stages, as well as the most convenient times, to discuss case progress.

Resolving Disputes It is important to discuss in advance what mechanisms you'll use if problems arise during the course of the lawyer's employment. This can be as difficult as writing a separation agreement on the eve of your wedding.

You can include a clause that states that you and your attorney will discuss openly all causes of dissatisfaction and seek reconciliation. You should specify that no fee is to be charged for time spent trying to resolve problems. You may also choose to specify that if this informal method of resolution fails, you will resolve the dispute through formal mechanisms, such as mediation or arbitration.

MAKING A CHOICE

When all interviews are completed, balance each lawyer's strengths and weaknesses, deciding which factors are most important to you and whether you have a clear choice. When choosing a malpractice lawyer, be careful to listen to how much it will probably cost to handle the case and exactly how much you are likely to win. Get the opinion of at least two attorneys.

If none of the lawyers you interview meets your needs, look for other prospects by drawing up a new list. Unless you are under extreme pressure to resolve your case quickly, it is far better to invest additional time at this stage than to try to undo a poor decision later.

Once you have made your choice, call the lawyer and make an appointment to spell out the final terms of employment and fees and to get them in writing. Be sure you get a copy of the final agreement, with original signatures.

CHAPTER 3

TRENDS AND STATISTICS

In 1986 the American Bar Association's National Legal Malpractice Data Center analyzed 29,227 legal malpractice claims filed with insurance carriers. Experts in malpractice believe that the trends reported in this study will remain constant for many years. This chapter reports information from that study, including what kinds of claims are filed, who they are usually against and the amounts of their settlements. It is important to note that the study did not include malpractice claims against lawyers who do not carry malpractice insurance.

The number of legal malpractice claims has increased dramatically since the early 1970s. Figure 1 shows the increase in the number of decisions by courts of appeals. Because few claims make it to court, much less to the appeals level, this table is evidence of the growing tip of an even more rapidly growing iceberg.

CLAIMS FILED

The ABA study divided the kinds of claims into two categories: the areas of law that gave rise to the claims, and the type of misconduct alleged in them. The two areas of law most likely to give rise to a malpractice claim were found to be

Figure 1. Relative Frequency of Legal Malpractice Actions*

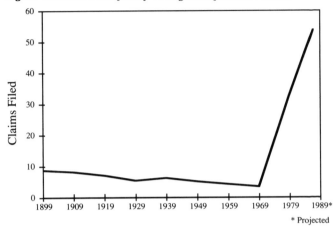

* Projected

*Reprinted from R. E. Mallen and J. M. Smith, *Legal Malpractice* (West Publishing Co., © 1989).

personal injury (typically handled for a contingency fee) and real estate law (Figure 2).

Personal injury cases ranged from "slip-and-fall" claims to claims against manufacturers alleging injury from a product. Real estate law cases ranged from complex property deals to the simple purchase of a house or condominium. Family law cases included such areas as divorce, child custody, adoption and prenuptial agreements. Estates, trust and probate cases involved distributing property through wills and trusts.

The two types of misconduct most complained about were "substantive errors" (failure to know or apply the law correctly) or "administrative errors" (missing deadlines, clerical mistakes, etc.) (Figure 3).

"Administrative" misconduct includes such errors as losing files, failing to return papers or telephone calls and clerical errors. "Substantive" misconduct includes such errors as failing to know or use the law, inadequate investigation and failing to know about a deadline. "Client relations" misconduct includes such errors as failing to follow a client's

Figure 2. Misconduct Claims by Area of Law*

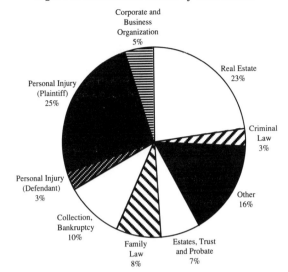

*Reprinted from R. E. Mallen and J. M. Smith, *Legal Malpractice (West Publishing Co., © 1989)*.

Figure 3. Types of Misconduct Claimed*

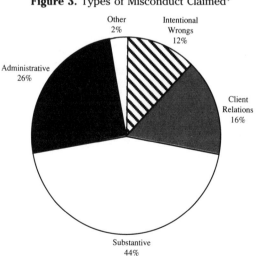

*Reprinted from R. E. Mallen and J. M. Smith, *Legal Malpractice* (West Publishing Co., © 1989).

instructions and quitting the case without properly informing the client or the court. "Intentional wrongs" include lying
about the case, theft, discrimination based on race or sex
and improper use of the legal process.

One legal scholar who analyzed the ABA's data drew the
conclusion that about 40 percent of all claims were related
to how the lawyer handled fees. This same analyst estimated
that another 25 percent of claims in the sample involved
complaints that the lawyer neglected or otherwise mishandled the client-attorney relationship.

WHOM CLAIMS ARE FILED AGAINST

The ABA study also offers demographic information about
the lawyers who have claims filed against them. Figures 4
and 5 show the percentage of claims against lawyers by size
of law firm and by years of experience practicing law. The
data also indicate that the larger law firms were less likely to
be charged with malpractice. And, contrary to popular opin-

Figure 4. Misconduct Claims by Firm Size*

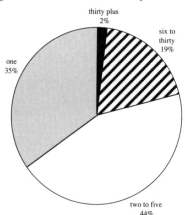

*Reprinted from R. E. Mallen and J. M. Smith, *Legal Malpractice* (West Publishing Co., © 1989).

Figure 5. Alleged Errors by Experience of Lawyer*

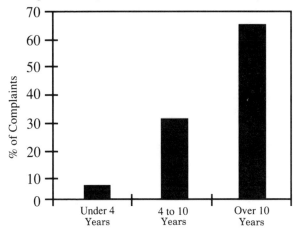

*Reprinted from R. E. Mallen and J. M. Smith, *Legal Malpractice* (West Publishing Co., © 1989).

ion, lawyers with the fewest years of experience were not found in this sample to be those most likely to be charged with misconduct.

HOW MUCH PEOPLE COLLECT

The ABA study also analyzed information about the outcomes of closed claims. (See Figures 6 and 7.) It calculated how many cases went to court, how many were settled, how many were dismissed and the amounts clients received. It reported that:

- Clients received no compensation in 63.3 percent of the claims.
- Fewer than 30 percent of the claims led to lawsuits.
- Clients who don't settle win only 1.2 percent of the time.
- Extremely few clients ever receive compensation over $1,000.

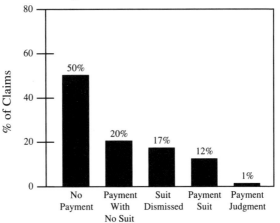

Figure 6. Outcome of Claims*

*Reprinted from *Profile of Legal Malpractice* (American Bar Association, © 1986).

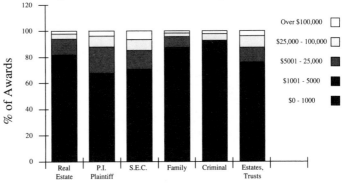

Figure 7. Amount Paid Claimant by Area of Law*

*Reprinted from R. E. Mallen and J. M. Smith, *Legal Malpractice* (West Publishing Co., © 1989).

THE FUTURE

ABA officials predict that claims for lawyer misconduct will continue to increase by as much as 20 percent a year. Not surprisingly, malpractice insurance premiums are also increasing, causing many lawyers to drop their coverage.

Although the increase in claims means that more clients are receiving compensation for at least some of their losses caused by lawyer misconduct, the news is not all good. Clients end up paying the bill whenever costs, including insurance premiums, increase for their lawyers. In addition, at least one legal scholar suggests that lawyers who are afraid of malpractice claims may begin overlawyering to protect themselves from suit. This could increase competent service only marginally while greatly increasing the legal costs to clients.

Finally, as more lawyers go "bare" (without insurance), more wronged clients lose the option of filing insurance claims. If the lawyer has left town or filed for bankruptcy, this may mean the client has no way to recover losses. And without insurance coverage, even a lawyer who is solvent is more likely to force a complaining client into an expensive and drawn-out lawsuit rather than settle out of court and be stuck with the bill.

On the bright side, one expert predicts that laws and procedures may be simplified if lawyers keep getting sued for questionable judgments.

CHAPTER 4

PROVING YOUR CASE

This chapter will look at lawsuits filed by clients against lawyers. It will concentrate on the two most common legal grounds that are used by clients but will also briefly cover less common grounds.

Malpractice law is always in flux because it is based not on written law passed by legislatures, but on a body of common law—that is, on the precedents established in previous court decisions. The right to sue for malpractice has been recognized since 1796, but there has been a substantial increase in cases in recent years. That means the courts are constantly reformulating malpractice law. The good news is that the recent trend is to expand clients' rights to compensation.[1]

Because malpractice law comes from court precedents, each court is guided by the decisions or opinions of its own state courts. The law, therefore, varies from state to state, and the facts of your case *must* be weighed in light of *your state courts'* interpretations of the law.

THE TWO COMMON THEORIES

The most common grounds for which clients sue lawyers are that their case was handled negligently (a branch of tort

---

[1]See *Using a Law Library,* HALT, 1988, for help on checking your state court decisions.

law, much of which provides compensation for personal injuries) or that the terms of your client-attorney agreement were broken (breach of contract). Negligence and breach-of-contract actions are called "malpractice" cases and differ from suits based on consumer fraud statutes or on theories of intentional misconduct—such as theft, fraud or misrepresentation—both of which are discussed at the end of this chapter.

From the client's perspective, the primary difference between suing for negligence and suing for breach of contract is that the deadline for filing with the court may be different. (See "Defenses," below.)

Regardless of what tack you take, winning a case is far from easy. To prove either negligence or breach of contract, every state requires that you show that:

- You had a client-attorney relationship
- The lawyer acted in a way that violated a duty to you
- The lawyer's violation of that duty caused you injury
- You suffered monetary loss because of your injuries

THE CLIENT-ATTORNEY RELATIONSHIP

In most instances, you must give evidence that the lawyer was representing you personally in a legal matter at the time this matter was mishandled. However, a growing number of states also allow some "nonclients" to sue. Perhaps the most common example would be a beneficiary of a will who sues a lawyer who mishandled the drafting of the will. Although the beneficiary never hired the lawyer, a direct financial loss resulted from the malpractice.

It is usually easy to prove that a lawyer was representing you, especially if you have copies of bills you paid. Courts have even found the necessary relationship when no fee was charged. To establish that a relationship existed, you can:

- Get the lawyer to acknowledge handling your case.
- Produce a copy of your agreement or a bill.
- Testify or otherwise provide evidence that the lawyer gave you legal advice that amounted to more than casual social conversation. (For example, you could give evidence of the work done for you, such as paperwork.)
- Show you had a good reason to rely on the lawyer's promise to handle your legal matter.
- Show that the lawyer took legal actions in your name, whether or not hired by you.

BREACH OF DUTY

Courts have held that you have a right to expect your lawyer to use "ordinary" skill, knowledge and diligence—ordinary, that is, compared to other lawyers'. This is called a *reasonable-lawyer standard.*

If you have signed an employment agreement with the lawyer you are suing, it can expand or limit this duty. For example, your agreement may include a clause that requires that the task be completed within two months. If the matter was not completed in two months, this would be a breach of duty.[1] For the most part, however, even when you have a written agreement, it usually incorporates a "reasonable lawyer" standard.

You almost always need at least one expert witness to testify that your lawyer did not live up to the reasonable-lawyer standard. Your expert is key to supporting your claim that the lawyer's conduct was more serious than an "honest mistake" or a "mere error in judgment."

The only instance when you would not need an expert is when a court would consider the misconduct obvious. For

---

[1]For information about what is considered a breach of duty in specific areas of law, such as family or property law, refer to R. E. Mallen and J. M. Smith's volumes, *Legal Malpractice* (see Appendix VI), or investigate your state court's recent opinions.

example, a judge is likely to find that, no matter how many lawyers make a general practice of missing court filing deadlines, this conduct falls below minimum acceptable standards and is a breach of duty.

Each state uses one or more of four versions of the reasonable-lawyer standard: Your lawyer's performance will be compared to that of other lawyers in the locality, lawyers in the same state, lawyers nationwide, or lawyers nationwide who specialize in a particular area of law. States are only now beginning to recognize that lawyers often specialize and that their clients have a right to expect that specialists will be held to a higher, "expert" standard.

Your attorney's duty also includes an obligation to *follow your instructions "faithfully."* This requires, for example, that your attorney accept or turn down a settlement offer according to your wishes, even when the attorney believes your decision is not in your own best interest. The exception is that your attorney is *not* bound to follow your instructions on tactical and strategic decisions related to actual litigation or if what you suggest is illegal.

There is a clear breach of duty if:
- Many appointments, hearings or court dates were missed
- The client-attorney agreement was violated
- Appropriate research wasn't done
- The filing deadline (statute of limitations) was missed

There is not necessarily a breach of duty if:
- The lawyer made an "honest mistake" or "error in judgment"
- You lost the case
- The lawyer did not file an appeal
- The lawyer was disciplined for ethical violations

PROVING FAULT

You must also establish that you suffered an injury that was caused, at least in part, by your lawyer's breach of duty. Most states hold that although the lawyer does not have to be the only cause of your loss, the lawyer must be shown directly responsible for it. Lawyers would say you must prove that but for the lawyer's breach, a loss would not have occurred. In plain English, that translates to—prove it was the lawyer's fault.

Establishing "causation" can be either simple or almost impossible, depending on the misconduct involved. Be warned: A lawyer who defends against a malpractice claim will almost always argue that the misconduct was not directly related to the injury—that is, that the lawyer was not at fault.

To establish what lawyers call *proximate causation,* you must show that your lawyer's misconduct *directly caused your loss.* This can be quite difficult. Most state courts will not find direct causation in the following example:

> You are sued for a slip-and-fall accident outside your house. Your lawyer misses the court's filing deadline. As a result, you lose the case by default and owe money damages. Because of the court's ruling against you, your credit rating is impaired and you have to back out of various investment plans. You wish to sue the lawyer to get back the interest you would have made on your investments and the penalties you had to pay for withdrawing.

In addition to showing a direct connection between the misconduct and your loss, most states require that you show that the injury caused a financial loss. It's not good enough to show that you lost an opportunity, or that you experienced minimal or no monetary loss because of the misconduct. You must provide evidence of *current* financial losses.

Other states lean toward principles of contract law. In those, you need show only slight damages, or that your agreement, whether written or oral, was violated. Proving that the contract was broken is enough to give you a right to nominal compensation. (These states also differ on the deadline for filing a lawsuit. See "Defenses," below.)

If you're claiming that your lawyer prepared legal documents incompetently, it will often be easy to show how that caused a loss and in what amount. For example, if your lawyer prepared a real estate lease incorrectly, it's fairly easy to attach a dollar value to the loss you suffered.

On the other hand, if you're claiming that you lost at trial because your lawyer was incompetent, in most states you will have to prove that you would have won if the lawyer had been competent. This puts the burden on you to prepare for a "trial within the trial"—proving your original case as well as the incompetence. For example, if you're challenging your lawyer's litigation skills or knowledge of the law, in effect you'll have to prove both that the lawyer was guilty of a breach of duty and that your case was solid enough that you would have received more money if not for that breach.

If your case fits this category, be warned: Proving two cases can be extremely expensive, and it gives you two chances of losing. Moreover, as discussed in the next section, lawyers often defend themselves by claiming that their clients didn't pursue all possible legal avenues to minimize their losses in the original case and therefore don't deserve full compensation.

GETTING COMPENSATED

If you've proven that your lawyer was guilty of malpractice, you have a right to financial reimbursement for your losses. Here we examine only the general types of compensation you can collect. You will need to check, or have a lawyer check for you, court decisions for specifics that apply in your state.

In general, courts will compensate you for the following losses:

Direct Economic Losses   Economic losses are those for which you can show bills, receipts or other financial statements. These can include lost interest, bills for hiring a lawyer to redo the work and paying back fees for needless or harmful legal work. In addition, you are entitled to compensation for any financial benefit you would have received if not for the misconduct, including the amount you would have won in court, or received if your lawyer had settled the case appropriately.

Foreseeable Losses   Most states allow you to recover any monetary losses your lawyer should have foreseen. For example, you can be compensated for an increase in insurance premiums you had to pay, or for the costs of restarting your business, if you can show that these costs were the result of the malpractice.

Statutory Damages   Some state legislatures have passed laws that supplement the losses you're allowed under court precedents (common law). Typically these provide for nominal damages ($1 or some other small token of "winning"), triple damages in cases of intentional misconduct, and the right to collect "extraordinary" damages in cases that involve theft.

Most states will not compensate you for the following.

Avoidable Losses   Clients have a legal obligation to minimize their losses. Almost every lawyer will attempt to decrease the amount of compensation owed by claiming that the client could have avoided, or mitigated, the losses. Because the legal system is such a maze of complexities, this defense may be particularly inviting in legal malpractice cases.

In one case, a court refused to compensate a client for the purchase price of a motel even though the real estate lawyer who negotiated the deal had failed to uncover a mortgage debt that caused the client to lose the property. The court reasoned that the client had had an opportunity to pay off the mortgage to minimize the loss and then sue the lawyer for damages, but had failed to do so.

In practical terms, protecting yourself from this defense usually means hiring still another lawyer to handle the on-going work on your original legal matter. This way you can prove you are doing everything to "avoid" additional losses. Your malpractice lawyer probably will not agree to handle both cases, because if called as a witness on the status of the original case, that lawyer would then have to withdraw as your malpractice lawyer.

Legal Malpractice Fees   Generally you cannot be reimbursed for your malpractice lawyer's fees. However, you can get compensated for any fees you have to pay to redo the original legal work.

Emotional Losses   In personal injury cases, the law usually allows you to recover money for such psychological injuries as "pain and suffering" and "mental anguish." Although the law is still evolving in this area, you usually cannot get money for these "noneconomic" damages in legal malpractice cases. (For special circumstances where that is possible, see "Other Theories for Suing," below.)

Speculative Losses   You cannot be compensated for injuries that were not foreseeable or that were caused primarily by something other than your lawyer's misconduct. The casual connection is not considered direct enough. For example, although you could recover for increased auto insurance premiums if your lawyer negligently defended your traffic collision case, you probably could not recover for lost wages if losing your auto insurance was only the last straw that prompted your boss to fire you.

Duplicate Compensation   In most states, if you receive compensation from one source, such as by winning an appeal of your original case or receiving compensation from the lawyer's insurance, you cannot also receive compensation for the same loss directly from the lawyer guilty of misconduct. If there is an appeal, however, you would be able to charge the cost of appealing the case to the lawyer who had mishandled it to begin with.

DEFENSES

Even though you prove your lawyer is guilty of malpractice, the lawyer can and will try to reduce the compensation owed. We have already discussed how the lawyer will usually claim the malpractice did not directly cause the injury and that the client failed to mitigate the losses. It usually does not work for the lawyer to use the defenses that the client was partly at fault (contributory negligence), that the client knew the risk of misconduct (assumed the risk) or that the client signed a valid release.

However, lawyers do have at their disposal an effective and often-used defense that you should know about.

Statute of Limitations   The only routine defense successfully used in malpractice cases is that your malpractice suit was filed too late, in violation of the statute of limitations. If your lawyer successfully shows that you missed the deadline for filing suit, your case will be dismissed by the court.

If your lawyer has any basis to assert a statute-of-limitations defense, chances are you are headed for complex litigation on the issue. Statute-of-limitations laws vary from state to state. Typically, they set deadlines that range from

one to six years. In almost every state, the deadline is based
on whether the court characterizes your case as a contract
or tort claim. If it's a contract claim, a longer limitation will
apply.

Once the deadline is determined, the court must figure out
when the clock began to run. Some courts have ruled that
it begins when the misconduct occurred, others when the
injury began, and still others when the lawyer's representation in the matter ended. In some instances, courts have
even held that the statute's clock does not begin to run until
the client knows or should know about the injury (called the
discovery rule).

OTHER THEORIES FOR SUING

Although the most common theories for suing are negligence and breach of contract, you might be able to sue your
lawyer for intentional misconduct or violation of your state's
consumer fraud statute.

Intentional misconduct includes stealing money, lying
about the case and misrepresenting facts in a way that
causes you to lose money. Suits for intentional lawyer misconduct are no different from other suits for intentional
misconduct and usually are based on the lawyer's lying
about facts to your financial detriment.

If you have good evidence of intentional misconduct, such
as theft, your lawyer is likely to leave town to avoid being
prosecuted by the police and sued by you. If your lawyer
was an uninsured solo practitioner and doesn't have any
property, you are probably out of luck. If your lawyer did
have malpractice insurance or was a member of a law firm,
however, the insurance or the law firm might be legally
required to compensate you for the losses. Be sure you
explore these options for compensation.

In recent years some courts have allowed clients' claims

under state consumer fraud statutes—often called "deceptive and unfair trade" laws. Although every state has a fraud law, in many states lawyers are exempt. In states where these laws have been applied to lawyers, courts have usually applied them to the so-called entrepreneurial aspects of law practice—actions taken to get or retain business. So, claims of deceptive billing or advertising practices have a chance of succeeding while issues of "professional conduct" such as competence probably do not. Since this area of law is evolving rapidly, be sure to explore the possibility of adding a consumer fraud violation to your suit.

CHAPTER 5

YOUR LAWYER'S INSURANCE

Lawyers can buy malpractice insurance from private companies or, in some states, through their state bar association. If a lawyer carries insurance, there is some chance that even if the lawyer is bankrupt or leaves town, there will be money to pay your claim.

Yet, that information is less reassuring than it sounds. In the first place, more than 40 percent of lawyers do not carry malpractice insurance. In addition, insurance companies are no more anxious to give you money than your lawyer is. They will sometimes deny that the lawyer is insured against the kind of misconduct you are alleging; they may also claim that no misconduct occurred.

Furthermore, you have no right to make a claim on your own against your lawyer's insurance company. Only your lawyer can do that. And many policies include a provision allowing the lawyer to demand that the insurer defend a claim, even if the lawyer's liability seems clear.

To determine whether your claim is covered by your lawyer's insurance, you need information about the insurance policy. In particular, find out:

Who Is Insured? Most insurance policies cover both your lawyer and employees of the lawyer or law firm, including paralegals and legal secretaries. Depending on your case and the insurance policy, expect the insurance company to argue that the work was done by someone who is not covered, such as an outside lawyer hired as an expert by your lawyer.

What Claims Are Within the Insured Period?
Whether your claim is covered by your lawyer's insurance can depend on whether it covers misconduct that occurred before the policy started. A very few policies cover misconduct that happened during the life of the policy regardless of whether the lawyer still carries the coverage when the client makes a claim. These are called *occurrence* policies. (Obviously, your claim must still be made within the statute of limitations.)

Under the most common kind of policy (a *claims-made policy*), your claim must be made during the life of the policy. So, if the lawyer retires and discontinues the insurance policy, your malpractice claim is not covered. Worse yet, some claims-made policies have a clause that excludes misconduct that occurred before the policy began. This provides skimpy coverage indeed, and is under challenge in some states for being against public policy.

What Is the Policy's Dollar Limit?
All insurance policies cap their coverage at a certain dollar amount. A typical limit for a small to medium-size law firm is $100,000 for any one claim and $3 million for all claims within a given year. Larger firms have limits up to $15 million. Under a claims-made policy, the dollar limit that will apply is the one in effect when the claim is made, not when the misconduct occurred.

What Are the "Notice" Requirements?
Many policies require that the lawyer notify the insurer of a malpractice claim within a specified period after learning about it. So if you file suit for malpractice and the court notifies your lawyer, but the lawyer fails to notify the insurance carrier in writing within the period of time specified in the policy, the insurance company may deny coverage.

If you know your lawyer's insurance company, you can send it copies of your notice of claim. Unfortunately, you have no easy way of finding out who your lawyer's insurance carrier is if the lawyer won't tell you. No law or bar rule requires the lawyer to divulge this information.

What Kinds of Misconduct or Compensation Are Excluded? Most policies cover any lawyer misconduct that occurs while the lawyer is practicing law. Although policy language may differ, all policies follow that essential line. Most policies have standard exclusions, however. These include:

Fraud and Other Intentional Misconduct Most malpractice insurance does not cover lying, stealing and other intentional misconduct. In other words, the more outrageous the lawyer's misconduct, the less likely the lawyer's insurance will cover your claim.

In some instances you may be able to present your claim in a way that it is covered by the lawyer's insurance. For example, if your lawyer hasn't paid you your share of a settlement check, instead of claiming theft you could claim that the lawyer breached the contract by failing to pay the money to you.

This exclusion can create an unusual twist. You may find that the insurance company, which is representing the lawyer, is arguing that the lawyer was an even worse culprit than you claim. In this example, you could find yourself fighting against the insurance company's insistence that your lawyer was a blatant thief.

Problems also occur when a malpractice claim includes a mix of both negligence and intentional misconduct. For example, if your lawyer missed a deadline for filing suit, then lied to you about it, the insurance company will not compensate you for the consequences of the lying, only for the consequences of missing the deadline. How insurance companies decide who pays what in such mixed cases is a complicated and still evolving area of law.

Work Not Considered Practicing Law   Insurance policies do not cover misconduct by lawyers when they are serving in a nonlawyer capacity—as a notary public, for example, or as a trustee in a bankruptcy case or an officer of a corporation. The lawyer may still be liable under malpractice law, but not covered by the insurance policy.

Distinguishing between practicing law and performing nonlawyer tasks can be quite complex, particularly in financial transactions when lawyers play multiple roles, some of which have to do with practicing law, others of which do not. The rule of thumb for insurance purposes is that if the lawyer was hired primarily to give legal advice, incidental nonlegal functions are covered by the insurance; but if the lawyer was hired primarily for nonlegal services, such as investing money, beware: Misconduct is usually not covered by the lawyer's insurance.

Bodily Injury or Mental Anguish   In one case, a lawyer and client were both in a plane crash that was clearly the fault of the lawyer, who had been piloting the plane. The trip had been necessary to complete legal work. The courts found that the insurance company did not have to compensate the client for injuries suffered in the crash, however, because bodily injury and mental distress are not considered part of claims based on the client-attorney relationship.

Refunding Lawyers' Fees   Insurance policies will not refund your lawyers' fees on the theory that it is the lawyer who collected them and the lawyer who should refund them. In legal language, the lawyer is considered to have been "unjustly enriched" by the fees, so the lawyer should "disgorge" them. Courts have also found other instances in which you are owed a refund of money that "unjustly enriched" the lawyer but must recover it directly from the lawyer, not the insurer.

Securities-Related Work   Many policies explicitly exclude coverage for legal work that involves stocks, bonds, or securities law. This is because securities-related claims usually involve multi-million-dollar awards.

When you know what is excluded from coverage, you will have a better idea of whether your claim is covered by your lawyer's insurance or not. This usually makes a difference in how you decide to present (or, in legalese, *frame*) your claim. However, even if your lawyer's insurance does include coverage for your kind of claim, you may have to file suit to get the money. Remember: Under most policies the lawyer has the right to demand that the insurance company defend against the claim and not settle, regardless of how clear the lawyer's liability appears to be.

CONCLUSION

The directory that follows is a compilation of the names and addresses of lawyers who take legal malpractice cases. It was gathered to help you pursue such a claim because we believe that every client should have the right to compensation when injured by a lawyer. Before you seek a lawyer to represent you in a malpractice suit, however, you should evaluate the following factors in regard to your case:

1. *It may still be difficult* to find a lawyer who is willing to take your case, though that situation is improving.
2. *Malpractice suits can be quite expensive* because you may have to pay for:
   - A malpractice lawyer
   - Expert witnesses
   - A second attorney to handle your original claim
   - Two trials in one
3. *Approximately 60 percent of all lawyers* have malpractice insurance that may cover at least some of your losses.
4. *You must carefully calculate* the economic probabilities and make sure what you may win is worth risking the expense of losing.
5. *Your lawyer will almost certainly try* to get out of paying you for your losses by claiming that:
   - The misconduct was an "error in judgment," not malpractice.

• The misconduct did not cause your loss.
• You could have minimized the injury and did not.

6. *Malpractice laws are changing,* and the changes are expanding consumers' rights.

The options available to clients to deal with lawyer misconduct—including malpractice suits—are inadequate. Change is obviously needed and may, in fact, be on its way. It is, however, crucial that consumers of legal services participate in the design of such changes.

DIRECTORY OF LEGAL MALPRACTICE ATTORNEYS

In this directory, states are listed in alphabetical order. Within each state, cities are listed alphabetically, and within each city, attorneys are listed alphabetically.

The lawyers listed are not approved by HALT or the publisher, and their services are not guaranteed. With few exceptions, most of them handle a variety of cases in addition to legal malpractice. For more information on how the directory was compiled, the sources from which the names were taken and how to shop for a malpractice lawyer, please refer to the introductory chapters.

ALABAMA

Allen W. Howell
Shinbaum, Thiemonge &
  Howell
P.O. Box 201
Montgomery, AL 36101-0201
(205) 269-4440

ALASKA

Charles D. Silvey
Staley, DeLisio, Cook & Sherry
714 4th Ave., Suite 200
Fairbanks, AK 99701
(907) 452-1855

ARIZONA

Gregory A. Bartolomei
Barry H. Hart, Ltd.
4350 E. Camelback Rd.,
  Suite 220B
Phoenix, AZ 85018
(602) 952-1777

Pasquale R. Cheche
Pasquale R. Cheche, P.C.
1430 E. Missouri Ave.,
  Suite 200
Phoenix, AZ 85014
(602) 264-0673

Carol C. Cure
O'Connor & Cavanagh
1 E. Camelback Rd., Suite 1100
Phoenix, AZ 85012
(602) 263-2652

Barry H. Hart
Barry H. Hart, Ltd.
4350 E. Camelback Rd.,
    Suite 220B
Phoenix, AZ 85018
(602) 952-1777

Roger A. McKee
Law Office of Roger A. McKee
1444 N. 16th St.
Phoenix, AZ 85006-3097
(602) 253-7253

Jay A. Zweig
Gallagher & Kennedy, P.A.
2600 N. Central Ave.,
    Suite 1800
Phoenix, AZ 85004
(602) 530-8000

William W. Edwards
Jones, Edwards, Smith &
    Kofron, P.C.
5151 E. Broadway, Suite 1600
Tucson, AZ 85711
(602) 747-4500

John G. Stompoly
Stompoly & Stroud, P.C.
1 S. Church Ave., Suite 1600
P.O. Box 3017
Tucson, AZ 85702-3017
(602) 628-8700

William G. Walker
Stompoly & Stroud, P.C.
1 S. Church Ave., Suite 1600
P.O. Box 3017
Tucson, AZ 85702-3017
(602) 628-8700

ARKANSAS

Arthur L. Allen
Allen Law Firm
400 W. Capitol, Suite 1700
Little Rock, AR 72201
(501) 375-5040

Winslow Drummond
McMath Law Firm, P.A.
711 W. 3rd St.
Little Rock, AR 72201
(501) 376-3021

Timothy O. Dudley
Wilson, Engstrom, Corum &
    Dudley
P.O. Box 71
Little Rock, AR 72203-0071
(501) 375-6453

Phillip H. McMath
McMath Law Firm, P.A.
711 W. 3rd St.
Little Rock, AR 72201
(501) 376-3021

CALIFORNIA

James S. Rummonds
Rummonds, Clause & Mair
311 Bonita Dr.
Aptos, CA 95001
(408) 688-2911

William Campisi, Jr.
Law Office of William Campisi,
    Jr.
1950 Addison St., Suite 200
Berkeley, CA 94704
(415) 549-3112

David R. Cadwell
Cadwell & Kohn, L.C.
8530 Wilshire Blvd., Suite 505
Beverly Hills, CA 90211
(213) 274-7078

Thomas T. Anderson
Thomas T. Anderson &
  Associates
45-926 Oasis St.
Indio, CA 92201
(619) 347-3364

Elaine B. Alston
Copenbarger & Associates
18300 Von Karman Ave.,
  Suite 800
Irvine, CA 92715
(714) 474-7979

Paul D. Copenbarger
Copenbarger & Associates
18300 Von Karman Ave.,
  Suite 800
Irvine, CA 92715
(714) 474-7979

Timothy J. Kozel
Kozel & Rady
4180 La Jolla Village Dr.,
  Suite 400
La Jolla, CA 92037
(619) 458-9445

Nancy L. Rady
Kozel & Rady
4180 La Jolla Village Dr.,
  Suite 400
La Jolla, CA 92037
(619) 458-9445

Richard L. Katz
Law Office of Richard L. Katz
101 Larkspur Landing Cir.,
  Suite 223
Larkspur, CA 94939
(415) 925-1600

Robert W. Finnerty
Girardi, Keese & Crane
1126 Wilshire Blvd.
Los Angeles, CA 90017
(213) 977-0211

Robert Gentino
Law Office of Robert Gentino
6922 Hollywood Blvd.,
  Suite 500
Los Angeles, CA 90028
(213) 465-3265

Thomas V. Girardi
Girardi, Keese & Crane
1126 Wilshire Blvd.
Los Angeles, CA 90017
(213) 489-5330

Michael A. Hoberman
Spector, Buter, Hoberman &
  Buzard
11611 San Vicente Blvd.,
  Suite 820
Los Angeles, CA 90049
(213) 820-6700

Joel W. H. Kleinberg
Joel W. H. Kleinberg, P.C.
1 Wilshire Blvd., Suite 2420
Los Angeles, CA 90017
(213) 624-1990

Robert Mansell
Law Office of Robert Mansell
11755 Wilshire Blvd.,
  Suite 1770
Los Angeles, CA 90025
(213) 479-3993

James P. McCashin
McCashin & Associates
11150 W. Olympic Blvd.,
    Suite 900
Los Angeles, CA 90064
(213) 478-9844

Timothy D. Reuben
Resch, Polster, Alpert &
    Berger
10281 W. Pico Blvd., 3rd Floor
Los Angeles, CA 90064
(213) 277-4008

Steven J. Ruben
Selvin, Weiner & Ruben
2029 Century Park E.,
    Suite 1700
Los Angeles, CA 90067
(213) 277-1555

Fred Rucker
Rucker & Clarkson
12121 Wilshire Blvd., Suite 200
Los Angeles, CA 90025
(213) 207-8696

Henry Seligsohn
King & Seligsohn
3550 Wilshire Blvd., Suite 1518
Los Angeles, CA 90010-1399
(213) 387-3204

David L. Sharp
Law Offices of David L. Sharp
1 Wilshire Blvd., Suite 1700
624 S. Grand Ave.
Los Angeles, CA 90017
(213) 623-5578

Steven Kazan
Kazan, McClain, Edises &
    Simon
171 12th St., 3rd Floor
Oakland, CA 94607
(415) 465-7728

Robert G. Schock
Law Offices of Robert G.
    Schock
200 Webster St., Suite 300
Oakland, CA 94607-3789
(415) 839-7722

Bobby D. Youngblood
Law Offices of Bobby D.
    Youngblood
1442 E. Lincoln Ave., Suite 359
Orange, CA 92665
(714) 998-5546

Dennis N. Westerberg
Dennis N. Westerberg, L.C.
2893 Sunrise Blvd., Suite 112
Rancho Cordova, CA 95742
(916) 638-1506

Gary B. Callahan
Wilcoxen, Callahan,
    Montgomery & Harbison
2114 K St.
Sacramento, CA 95816
(916) 442-2777

Joseph F. Harbison, III
Wilcoxen, Callahan,
    Montgomery & Harbison
2114 K St.
Sacramento, CA 95816
(916) 442-2777

D. Jack Haycock
Haycock & Pomykala
801 12th St., Suite 500
Sacramento, CA 95814
(916) 446-1517

James R. Montgomery
Wilcoxen, Callahan,
  Montgomery & Harbison
2114 K St.
Sacramento, CA 95816
(916) 442-2777

Daniel E. Wilcoxen
Wilcoxen, Callahan,
  Montgomery & Harbison
2114 K St.
Sacramento, CA 95816
(916) 442-2777

David R. Cadwell
Cadwell & Kohn, L.C.
1010 2nd Ave., Suite 1909
San Diego, CA 92101
(619) 236-9976

Dickran A. Semerdjian
Post, Kirby, Noonan & Sweat
701 B St., Suite 1400
San Diego, CA 92101
(619) 231-8666

Mark Abelson
Campagnoli, Abelson &
  Campagnoli
120 Montgomery St.,
  Suite 1825
San Francisco, CA 94104
(415) 421-1515

Jennifer Becker
Starnes & Drapiewski
333 Hayes St., 2nd Floor
San Francisco, CA 94102
(415) 863-4443

Paul F. Bennett
David B. Gold, P.C.
595 Market St., Suite 2300
San Francisco, CA 94105
(415) 777-2230

Richard D. Bridgman
Law Offices of Richard D.
  Bridgman
350 California St., Suite 1470
San Francisco, CA 94104
(415) 956-6090

Stephen T. Cox
Hoberg, Finger, Brown, Cox &
  Molligan
703 Market St., Suite 1800
San Francisco, CA 94103
(415) 543-9464

James A. Dorskind
Friedman, Sloan & Ross, P.C.
1 Maritine Plaza, Suite 1040
San Francisco, CA 94111
(415) 788-2201

Daniel Drapiewski
Starnes & Drapiewski
333 Hayes St., 2nd Floor
San Francisco, CA 94102
(415) 863-4443

John M. Feder
Rouda, Feder & Tietjen
465 California St., Suite 210
San Francisco, CA 94104
(415) 398-5398

B. Mark Fong
Robert A. Harlem, Inc. &
  Associates
120 Montgomery St.,
  Suite 2410
San Francisco, CA 94104
(415) 981-1801

Paul A. Frassetto
Law Office of Paul A. Frassetto
101 Vallejo St.
San Francisco, CA 94111
(415) 433-6790

Robert A. Harlem
Robert A. Harlem, Inc. &
  Associates
120 Montgomery St.,
  Suite 2410
San Francisco, CA 94104
(415) 981-1801

Thomas J. LoSavio
Low, Ball & Lynch
601 California St., 21st Floor
San Francisco, CA 94108
(415) 981-6630

Ronald E. Mallen
Long & Levit
101 California St., Suite 2300
San Francisco, CA 94111
(415) 397-2222

Peter N. Molligan
Hoberg, Finger, Brown, Cox &
  Molligan
703 Market St., Suite 1800
San Francisco, CA 94103
(415) 543-9464

David W. Moyer
Hoberg, Finger, Brown, Cox &
  Molligan
703 Market St., Suite 1800
San Francisco, CA 94103
(415) 543-9464

Ronald H. Rouda
Rouda, Feder & Tietjen
465 California St., Suite 210
San Francisco, CA 94104
(415) 398-5398

Tanya Starnes
Starnes & Drapiewski
333 Hayes St., 2nd Floor
San Francisco, CA 94102
(415) 863-4443

Theresa M. Stewart
Howard, Rice, Nemerovski,
  Canady, Robertson & Falk
3 Embarcadero Center
San Francisco, CA 94111
(415) 434-1600

Timothy Tietjen
Rouda, Feder & Tietjen
465 California St., Suite 210
San Francisco, CA 94104
(415) 398-5398

David P. Weaver, Jr.
Law Offices of David P.
  Weaver, Jr.
160 Sansome St., Suite 1100
San Francisco, CA 94104
(415) 981-1906

Guy A. Wilson
Worthington & Worthington
1 Embarcadero Center,
  Suite 370
San Francisco, CA 94111
(415) 982-8880

Michael G. Ackerman
Popelka, Allard, McCowan &
  Jones
160 W. Santa Clara St.,
  Suite 1300
San Jose, CA 95115-0036
(408) 298-6610

Robert B. Ingram
Law Office of Robert B. Ingram
4340 Redwood Hwy., Suite 352
San Rafael, CA 94903
(415) 499-0800

Randy H. McMurray
Greene, Broillet, Taylor &
  Wheeler
100 Wilshire Blvd., 21st Floor
Santa Monica, CA 90401-1110
(213) 576-1200

Phillip Feldman
Law Offices of Phillip Feldman
15250 Ventura Blvd., Suite 604
Sherman Oaks, CA 91403-3287
(818) 986-9890

Lane S. Kay
Law Offices of Phillip Feldman
15250 Ventura Blvd., Suite 604
Sherman Oaks, CA 91403-3287
(818) 986-9890

Donald S. Bayne
Bayne & Bayne
14530 Delano St., Suite 100
Van Nuys, CA 91411
(818) 781-2800

John M. Bayne, Jr.
Bayne & Bayne
14530 Delano St., Suite 100
Van Nuys, CA 91411
(818) 781-2800

R. Kenneth Bauer
Law Offices of R. Kenneth
  Bauer
500 Ygnacio Valley Rd.,
  Suite 250
Walnut Creek, CA 94596
(415) 942-3099

COLORADO

Paul Snyder, Jr.
Brauchli & Snyder
1401 Walnut St., Suite 400
Boulder, CO 80302
(303) 443-1118

John G. Taussig, Jr.
Taussig & Taussig
1919 14th St., Suite 805
Boulder, CO 80302
(303) 449-9576

Robert E. Benson
Holland & Hart
555 17th St., Suite 2900
Denver, CO 80202
(303) 295-8234

Michael S. Burg
Burg & Eldredge, P.C.
4643 S. Ulster St., Suite 900
Denver, CO 80237
(303) 779-5595

Roger T. Castle
Roger T. Castle, P.C.
1888 Sherman St., Suite 415
Denver, CO 80203
(303) 839-8251

Herbert W. DeLaney, Jr.
Herbert W. DeLaney, Jr., P.C.
50 S. Steele St., Suite 588
Denver, CO 80209
(303) 329-0540

Peter B. Goldstein
Peter B. Goldstein, A.A.L.
303 E. 17th Ave., Suite 850
Denver, CO 80203
(303) 860-8200

John A. Kintzele
Law Office of John A. Kintzele
1317 Delaware St.
Denver, CO 80204
(303) 892-6494

William J. McCarren
Miller & McCarren, P.C.
370 17th St., Suite 3050
Denver, CO 80202
(303) 592-4444

Stuart Pack
Sherman & Howard
633 17th St., Suite 3000
Denver, CO 80202
(303) 299-8430

Larry D. Sather
Law Offices of Larry D. Sather
303 E. 17th Ave., Suite 920
Denver, CO 80203
(303) 831-4464

Jeffrey A. Springer
Springer & Steinberg, P.C.
1600 Broadway, Suite 1500
Denver, CO 80202
(303) 861-2800

Charles Welton
Charles Welton, P.C.
1751 Gilpin St.
Denver, CO 80218
(303) 333-8447

Michael R. Williams
Sherman & Howard
633 17th St., Suite 3000
Denver, CO 80202
(303) 297-2900

James K. Kreutz
Kreutz & Associates, P.C.
5655 S. Yosemite
Englewood, CO 80111
(303) 779-8224

Thomas J. Tomazion
Kreutz & Associates, P.C.
5655 S. Yosemite
Englewood, CO 80111
(303) 779-8224

CONNECTICUT

A. Patrick Alcarez
Regnier, Taylor, Curran &
    Eddy
60 Washington St.
Hartford, CT 06450
(203) 249-9121

A. Paul Spinella
Law Offices of A. Paul Spinella
60 Washington St.
Hartford, CT 06106
(203) 278-0804

DELAWARE

Howard M. Berg
Berg, Bifferato, Tighe, &
    Cottrell
P.O. Box 33
Wilmington, DE 19899-0033
(302) 571-8600

DISTRICT OF COLUMBIA

Christopher G. Hoge
Crowley, Hoge & Fein, P.C.
1219 Connecticut Ave. NW,
    Suite 400
Washington, DC 20036
(202) 296-7066

Doug Smith
Klimaski, Miller & Smith
1899 L St. NW, Suite 1250
Washington, DC 20036
(202) 296-5600

Barbara Sosnick
Law Office of Barbara Sosnick
305 H St. NW
Washington, DC 20001
(202) 289-6058

Marvin L. Szymkowicz
Law Firm of Allan I.
  Mendelsohn
1155 15th St. NW, Suite 400
Washington, DC 20005
(202) 296-1866

FLORIDA

F. Wallace Pope, Jr.
Johnson, Blakely, Pope, Bokor,
  Ruppel & Burns, P.A.
911 Chestnut St.
P.O. Box 1368
Clearwater, FL 34617-1368
(813) 461-1818

Sheridan Weissenborn
Papy, Weissenborn & Papy
201 Alhambra Cir., Suite 502
Coral Gables, FL 33134
(305) 446-5100

Samuel L. Heller
Samuel L. Heller, P.A.
1290 E. Oakland Park Blvd.,
  Suite 101
Ft. Lauderdale, FL 33334
(305) 566-6440

Lawrence P. Kuvin
Lawrence P. Kuvin &
  Associates, Inc.
P.O. Box 350276
Ft. Lauderdale, FL 33335-0276
(305) 524-4605

C.R. McDonald, Jr.
C.R. McDonald, Jr., P.A.
Treasure Coast Office Park,
  Suite D
3953 S. Federal Hwy.
Ft. Pierce, FL 34982
(407) 489-5700

Richard A. Barnett
Barnett & Hammer, P.A.
4651 Sheridan St., Suite 325
Hollywood, FL 33021
(305) 961-8550

Alan G. Greer
Floyd, Pearson, Richman,
  Greer, Weil, Brumbaugh &
  Russomanno, P.A.
Courthouse Ctr., 26th Floor
175 N.W. 1st Ave.
Miami, FL 33128
(305) 373-4000

Jeff Lloyd
Squire, Sanders & Dempsey
201 S. Biscayne Blvd.,
  Suite 3000
Miami, FL 33131
(305) 577-7765

Dennis G. Diecidue
Dennis G. Diecidue, P.A.
612 Horatio St.
Tampa, FL 33606
(813) 251-0203

Joseph Kinman
Shackleford, Farrior, Stallings
　& Evans, P.A.
P.O. Box 3324
Tampa, FL 33601-3324
(813) 273-5106

Robin Lane
Robin Lane, P.A.
3737 Neptune St.
Tampa, FL 33629
(813) 253-2229

Hugh N. Smith
Smith & Fuller, P.A.
101 E. Kennedy Blvd.,
　Suite 1800
Tampa, FL 33602
(813) 221-7171

Bill Wagner
Wagner, Cunningham,
　Vaughan & McLaughlin, P.A.
708 Jackson St.
Tampa, FL 33602
(813) 223-7421

Charles J. Cheves
Cheves, Rapkin & DiCiantis,
　P.A.
341 Venice Ave. W
Venice, FL 34285
(813) 485-7705

H. Michael Easley
Easley & Willits
1655 Palm Beach Lakes Blvd.,
　Suite 800
West Palm Beach, FL 33401
(407) 684-7300

Jeffrey M. Liggio
Law Office of Jeffrey M. Liggio
804 N. Olive Ave.
West Palm Beach, FL 33401
(407) 833-6604

Robert M. Montgomery, Jr.
Montgomery & Larmoyeux
P.O. Drawer 3086
West Palm Beach, FL
　33402-3086
(407) 832-2880

GEORGIA

Frank J. Beltran
Beltran & Coffey
1101 Peachtree Center Cain
　Tower
229 Peachtree St. NE
Atlanta, GA 30303-1676
(404) 658-1101

Myles E. Eastwood
Jones, Brown, Brennan &
　Eastwood
600 W. Peachtree St. NW,
　Suite 1900
Atlanta, GA 30308
(404) 872-5300

Lee S. Goldstein
Goldstein & Schatten, P.C.
1000 Parkwood Cir., Suite 470
Atlanta, GA 30339
(404) 988-0500

Carolyn R. Gorwitz
Bondurant, Mixson & Elmore
1201 W. Peachtree St.,
　Suite 3900
Atlanta, GA 30309
(404) 881-4110

Taylor W. Jones
Jones, Brown, Brennan &
 Eastwood
600 W. Peachtree St. NW,
 Suite 1900
Atlanta, GA 30308
(404) 872-5300

Jeffrey M. Smith
Arnall, Golden & Gregory
55 Park Pl., Suite 400
Atlanta, GA 30335
(404) 527-4690

Clifford Steele
Law Office of Clifford Steele
5505 Roswell Rd., Suite 3
Atlanta, GA 30342
(404) 255-2929

HAWAII

Robert B. Ingram
Sterns & Ingram
733 Bishop, Suite 2300
Honolulu, HI 96813
(808) 528-1900

Dennis W. Potts
Dennis W. Potts, A.A.L. A.L.C.
333 Queen St., Suite 805
Honolulu, HI 96813
(808) 537-4575

James Krueger
Law Offices of James Krueger
2065 Main St.
Wailuku, HI 96793-1648
(808) 244-7444

Steven B. Songstad
Law Office of Steven B.
 Songstad
2180 Main St., Suite 700
Wailuku, HI 96793
(808) 242-4936

IDAHO

Allen B. Ellis
Ellis, Brown & Sheils, Jr.
707 N. 8th St.
Boise, ID 83702
(208) 345-7832

Paul T. Clark
Clark & Feeney
The Train Station, Suite 201
13th & Main Sts.
P.O. Box 285
Lewiston, ID 83501-0285
(208) 743-9516

ILLINOIS

Hugh M. Talbert
Talbert & Mallon, P.C.
630 E. Broadway
P.O. Box 800
Alton, IL 62002-0800
(618) 465-4400

Gordon Arnett
Law Office of Gordon Arnett
5875 N. Lincoln Ave.
Chicago, IL 60659
(312) 334-0400

Paul P. Biebel
Winston & Strawn
35 W. Wacker Dr.
Chicago, IL 60601
(312) 558-5555

Charles A. Boyle
Charles A. Boyle & Associates,
   Ltd.
29 S. LaSalle St., Suite 345
Chicago, IL 60603
(312) 346-4944

Irving M. King
Cotton, Watt, Jones & King
122 S. Michigan Ave., Suite
   2050
Chicago, IL 60603
(312) 427-5100

John J. Lowrey
Lowrey & Smerz, Ltd.
100 W. Monroe St.
Chicago, IL 60603
(312) 332-5433

Robert H. Nichols
Cotton, Watt, Jones & King
122 S. Michigan Ave., Suite
   2050
Chicago, IL 60603
(312) 427-5100

Joseph M. O'Callaghan
O'Callaghan & Associates, P.C.
230 W. Monroe St.
Chicago, IL 60606
(312) 332-1600

Don H. Reuben
Winston & Strawn
35 W. Wacker Dr.
Chicago, IL 60601
(312) 558-5555

Gregory A. Stayart
Romanyak & Associates
111 W. Washington St.,
   Suite 1611
Chicago, IL 60602
(312) 807-4800

Jerome H. Torshen
Torshen, Schoenfield &
   Spreyer, Ltd.
105 W. Adams St., Suite 3200
Chicago, IL 60603
(312) 372-9282

Russell Woody
Cotton, Watt, Jones & King
122 S. Michigan Ave.,
   Suite 2050
Chicago, IL 60603
(312) 427-5100

Gary E. Peel
Peel & Dugan
2 Center Grove Rd.
Edwardsville, IL 62025
(618) 692-0500

George P. Troha
Troha, Troha & Bednarek, Ltd.
71 N. Chicago St.
Juliet, IL 60431
(815) 727-9271

Roger Zamparo, Jr.
Zamparo & Goldstein, P.C.
899 Skokie Blvd., Suite 300
Northbrook, IL 60062
(708) 564-3100

Vern L. Davitt
Law Office of Vern L. Davitt
504 N. Church St.
Rockford, IL 61103
(815) 965-9595

INDIANA

M. Robert Benson
Benson, Pantello, Morris &
   James
3505 Lake Ave.
Ft. Wayne, IN 46805
(219) 424-7077

William F. Conour
Conour & Doehrman
1 Indiana Sq., Suite 1725
Indianapolis, IN 46204
(317) 269-3550

Jon Pactor
Law Office of Jon Pactor
1 Indiana Sq., Suite 1725
Indianapolis, IN 46204
(317) 636-0686

Thomas R. Ruge
Ruge & Ruppert
101 W. Ohio, Suite 590
Indianapolis, IN 46204
(317) 684-3900

Robert J. Shula
Price & Shula
301 Massachusetts Ave.
Indianapolis, IN 46204
(800) 229-8787

IOWA

James Hood
James Hood Law Offices
302 Union Arcade Bldg.
Davenport, IA 52801
(319) 323-5255

Richard M. McMahon
Betty, Neunam & McMahon
600 Union Arcade Bldg.
111 E. 3rd St.
Davenport, IA 52801
(319) 326-4491

Roland D. Peddicord
Law Office of Roland D.
  Peddicord
218 6th Ave., Suite 300
P.O. Box 9130
Des Moines, IA 50306-9130
(515) 243-2100

Kenneth L. Keith
Keith, Orsborn, Milani &
  Neary
P.O. Box 218
Ottumwa, IA 52501-0218
(515) 682-5447

William J. Giles, IV
Giles & Giles
722 Frances Bldg.
Sioux City, IA 51101
(712) 252-4458

KANSAS

Stephen W. Brown
Megaffin & Brown
203 S. Main
Pratt, KS 67124
(316) 672-5626

Charles S. Fisher, Jr.
Fisher, Cavanaugh & Smith,
  P.A.
1035 Bank IV Tower
534 Kansas Ave.
Topeka, KS 66603
(913) 354-7622

Brock R. Snyder
Snyder Law Firm
1403 S.W. Topeka Blvd.
Topeka, KS 66612
(913) 232-1700

Richard D. Cordry
Cordry & Hartman
727 N. Waco, Suite 145
P.O. Box 47528
Wichita, KS 67201-7528
(316) 269-1423

KENTUCKY

Ann B. Oldfather
Oldfather & Morris
1 Mezzanine
304 W. Liberty St.
Louisville, KY 40202
(502) 589-5500

Lee Sitlinger
Sitlinger, McGlincy, Steiner &
    Theiler
3450 First National Tower
Louisville, KY 40202
(502) 589-2627

Gary Weiss
Weiss & Roseberry
510 W. Broadway St.
Louisville, KY 40202
(502) 587-1000

LOUISIANA

Oscar L. Shoenfelt, III
Moore, Walters & Shoenfelt
P.O. Box 2109
Baton Rouge, LA 70821-2109
(504) 344-2000

Edward J. Walters
Moore, Walters & Shoenfelt
P.O. Box 2109
Baton Rouge, LA 70821-2109
(504) 344-2000

Lamar M. Richardson, Jr.
Murray, Braden, Gonzalez &
    Richardson
1895 W. Causeway Approach
Mandeville, LA 70448
(504) 626-4414

Hugh D. Aldigé
Law Office of Hugh D. Aldigé
2901 Ridgelake Dr., Suite 113
Metairie, LA 70002
(504) 837-8555

James F. Willeford
Ryan & Willeford
201 St. Charles Ave., Suite 3701
New Orleans, LA 70170
(504) 582-1280

MAINE

Jeffrey A. Thaler
Berman, Simmons & Goldberg
129 Lisbon St.
Lewiston, ME 04240
(207) 784-3576

John G. Connor
Friedman & Babcock
6 City Ctr.
Portland, ME 04101
(207) 761-0900

MARYLAND

Warren D. Stephens
Law Offices of Warren D.
    Stephens, P.A.
198 West St.
Annapolis, MD 21401
(301) 280-3200

Richard Bardos
Sandbower, Gabler &
    O'Shaughnessy, P.A.
22 E. Fayette St.
Baltimore, MD 21215
(301) 576-0762

George E. Golomb
Law Office of George E.
  Golomb
111 S. Calvert St., Suite 2700
Baltimore, MD 21202
(301) 385-5261

Gary I. Strausberg
Janet & Strausberg
Executive Center at Hooks
  Lane
8 Reservoir Cir., Suite 200
Baltimore, MD 21208
(301) 653-3200

Gary A. Wais
Snyder, Baron, Mehlman &
  Wais
1829 Reisterstown Rd.,
  Suite 260
Baltimore, MD 21208
(301) 653-3700

David L. Scull
Law Offices of David L. Scull
8401 Connecticut Ave., PH-3
Chevy Chase, MD 20815
(301) 951-0100

Kevin J. McCarthy
McCarthy, Bacon & Costello
1801 McCormick Dr., Suite 410
Landover, MD 20785
(301) 925-1600

George W. Shadoan
Shadoan & Michael
108 Park Ave.
Rockville, MD 20850
(301) 762-5150

Jules Fink
Law Offices of Jules Fink
8720 Georgia Ave., Suite 1000
Silver Spring, MD 20910
(301) 585-0622

Coleen S. Clemente
Law Office of Coleen S.
  Clemente
8 N. Court St.
Westminster, MD 21157
(301) 848-9151

MASSACHUSETTS

Richard M. Howland
Richard M. Howland, P.C.
358 N. Pleasant St.
P.O. Box 2300
Amherst, MA 01004-2300
(413) 549-4570

Robert M. Buchanan
Sullivan & Worcester
1 Post Office Sq.
Boston, MA 02109
(617) 338-2861

Charles Cohen
Egan, Flanagan & Cohen, P.C.
67 Market St.
P.O. Box 9035
Springfield, MA 01102-9035
(413) 737-0260

Charles Danis, Jr.
Egan, Flanagan & Cohen, P.C.
67 Market St.
P.O. Box 9035
Springfield, MA 01102-9035
(413) 737-0260

John O. Mirick
Mirick, O'Connell, DeMallie &
    Lougee
1700 Mechanics Bank Tower
Worcester, MA 01608
(508) 799-0541

MICHIGAN

Thomas Blaske
Blaske & Blaske
320 N. Main St., Suite 303
Ann Arbor, MI 48104
(313) 747-7055

Barry Gates
L. Ray Bishop & Associates,
    P.C.
709 W. Huron
Ann Arbor, MI 48103
(313) 668-1606

E. Robert Blaske
Blaske & Blaske
1509 Comerica Tower
Battle Creek, MI 49017
(616) 964-9491

Anthony M. Calderone
Anthony M. Calderone, P.C.
391 S. Shore Dr., Suite 318
Battle Creek, MI 49015
(616) 962-9577

Robert A. Cole
Anthony M. Calderone, P.C.
391 S. Shore Dr., Suite 318
Battle Creek, MI 49015
(616) 962-9577

James L. Elsman
Law Offices of James L.
    Elsman
The Business Bldg.
635 Elm St.
Birmingham, MI 48009
(313) 645-0750

Robert S. Harrison
Robert S. Harrison &
    Associates
6735 Telegraph Rd., Suite 350
Birmingham, MI 48010
(313) 540-5900

Sheldon G. Larky
Law Office of Sheldon G. Larky
30600 Telegraph Rd.,
    Suite 2160
Birmingham, MI 48010
(313) 642-4660

Robert H. Janover
Law Offices of Robert H.
    Janover
860 W. Long Lake Rd.,
    Suite 200
Bloomfield Hills, MI 48302-2010
(313) 540-1620

Eric J. McCann
Eric J. McCann, P.C.
33 Bloomfield Hills Pkwy.,
    Suite 155
Bloomfield Hills, MI 48304
(313) 647-9505

David K. Barnes, Jr.
Sachs, Nunn, Kates, Kadushin,
    O'Hare, Helveston &
    Waldman, P.C.
1000 Farmer
Detroit, MI 48226
(313) 965-3464

Hugh M. Davis
Hugh M. Davis, P.C.
3146 Penobscot Bldg.
Detroit, MI 48226
(313) 961-2255

George M. DeGrood, III
Thomas, DeGrood & Witenoff,
   P.C.
960 Penobscot Bldg.
Detroit, MI 48226
(313) 964-5202

John L. Foster
Foster, Meadows & Ballard,
   P.C.
3200 Penobscot Bldg.
Detroit, MI 48226
(313) 961-3234

James M. Catchick
Law Offices of James M.
   Catchick
200 N. Division Ave.
Grand Rapids, MI 49503
(616) 459-3839

William G. Reamon
William G. Reamon, P.C.
200-C Waters Bldg.
Grand Rapids, MI 49503
(616) 774-2377

Stuart J. Dunnings, III
Dunnings & Frawley, P.C.
530 S. Pine St.
Lansing, MI 48933
(517) 487-8222

E. Nickolas Bridges
Bridges & Bridges
701 Teal Lake Ave.
Negaunee, MI 49866
(906) 475-9971

Arnold M. Gordon
Weinstein, Gordon & Hoffman,
   P.C.
18411 W. Twelve Mile Rd.
Southfield, MI 48076
(313) 443-1500

Lee I. Turner
Turner & Turner, P.C.
24901 Northwestern Hwy.,
   Suite 417
Southfield, MI 48075
(313) 355-1727

Paul A. Frumkin
Kemp, Klein, Endelman &
   Umphrey
201 W. Big Beaver Rd.,
   Suite 600
Troy, MI 48084
(313) 528-1111

MINNESOTA

John W. Carey
Sieben, Grose, Von Holtum,
   McCoy & Carey
117 S. Park St.
Fairfax, MN 55332
(507) 426-8211

Richard L. Pemberton
Hefte, Pemberton, Sorlie &
   Rufer
110 N. Mill St.
Fergus Falls, MN 56537
(218) 736-5493

James H. Manahan
Manahan Law Office
P.O. Box 287
Mankato, MN 56002-0287
(507) 387-5661

George E. Antrim, III
Krause & Rollins, Chtd.
310 Groveland Ave.
Minneapolis, MN 55403
(612) 874-8550

Craig A. Goudy
Cox & Goudy
600 A. Butler Sq.
Minneapolis, MN 55403
(612) 338-1414

Peter W. Riley
DeParcq, Hunegs, Stone,
   Koenig & Reid, P.A.
565 Northstar E
608 2nd Ave. S
Minneapolis, MN 55402
(612) 339-4511

Michael A. Stern
Fredrikson & Byron, P.A.
900 2nd Ave. S
Minneapolis, MN 55402
(612) 347-7024

Morley Friedman
Morley Friedman & Associates
2010 American National Bank
   Bldg.
101 E. 5th St.
St. Paul, MN 55101
(612) 228-1207

MISSISSIPPI

Charles M. Merkel
Merkel & Cocke
P.O. Box 1388
Clarksdale, MS 38614-1388
(601) 627-9641

MISSOURI

John J. Allan
McAvoy & Allan
558 Gravois Rd.
Fenton, MO 63026
(314) 436-3300

Jorge A. Elliott
Law Office of Jorge A. Elliott
Merchant Trust Ctr., Suite 500
1125 Grand Ave.
Kansas City, MO 64106
(816) 471-1064

J. William Turley
Williams, Robinson, Turley,
   Crump & White
P.O. Box 47
Rolla, MO 65401-0047
(314) 341-2266

Robert E. Rapp
Law Office of Robert E. Rapp
8008 Carondelet Ave.,
   Suite 301
St. Louis, MO 63105
(314) 727-9911

John Wallach
Hoffman & Wallach
1015 Locust St., Suite 1134
St. Louis, MO 63101
(314) 241-1020

MONTANA

Marcey Schwarz
Schwarz Law Firm, P.C.
P.O. Box 21386
Billings, MT 59104-1386
(406) 656-4409

NEBRASKA

Gregory D. Barton
Harding & Ogborn
P.O. Box 82028
Lincoln, NE 68501-2028
(402) 475-6761

NEVADA

Richard McKnight
Richard McKnight, Chtd.
330 S. 3rd St., Suite 900
Las Vegas, NV 89101
(702) 388-7185

NEW HAMPSHIRE

Kenneth G. Bouchard
Bouchard & Mallory, P.A.
100 Middle St.
Manchester, NH 03101
(603) 623-7222

Kenneth M. Brown
Kahn & Brown
187 Main St.
Nashua, NH 03060
(603) 882-1600

Lesley Cornell
Mulvey, Noucas & Cornell
P.O. Box 478
Portsmouth, NH 03801-0478
(603) 431-1333

NEW JERSEY

Anthony P. Ambrosio
Ambrosio, Kyreakakis &
  DiLorenzo
317 Belleville Ave.
Bloomfield, NJ 07003
(201) 748-7474

Donald Horowitz
Law Offices of Donald
  Horowitz
24 Bergen St.
Hackensack, NJ 07601
(201) 343-0100

Charles Rodgers
Breslin & Breslin
41 Main St.
Hackensack, NJ 07601
(201) 342-4014

Philip Rosenbach
Rosenbach & Rosenbach
66 W. Mount Pleasant Ave.
Livingston, NJ 07039
(201) 740-2262

Stephen Schnitzer
Stephen Schnitzer, P.A.
40 W. Northfield Rd.
P.O. Box 691
Livingston, NJ 07039-0691
(201) 533-1212

Hilton L. Stein
Law Offices of Hilton L. Stein
339 Main Rd.
Montville, NJ 07045
(201) 299-8858

Alvin D. Hersh
Hersh, Ramsey, Berman &
  Rockoff, P.C.
222 Ridgedale Ave.
P.O. Box 2249
Morristown, NJ 07962-2249
(201) 267-4880

Jeffry Mintz
Schlesinger, Mintz & Pilles
129 High St.
Mount Holly, NJ 08060
(609) 267-5400

Jan Schlesinger
Schlesinger, Mintz & Pilles
129 High St.
Mount Holly, NJ 08060
(609) 267-5400

Kenneth A. Berkowitz
Blume, Vazquez, Goldfaden,
    Berkowitz & Donnelly, P.C.
5 Commerce St.
Newark, NJ 07102-3989
(201) 622-1881

John M. Blume
Blume, Vazquez, Goldfaden,
    Berkowitz & Donnelly, P.C.
5 Commerce St.
Newark, NJ 07102-3989
(201) 622-1881

Dennis M. Donnelly
Blume, Vazquez, Goldfaden,
    Berkowitz & Donnelly, P.C.
5 Commerce St.
Newark, NJ 07102-3989
(201) 622-1881

Oliver Lofton
Lofton & Wolfe
18 Beaver St.
Newark, NJ 07102
(201) 621-1800

Joe Maran
Maran & Maran
Legal Center, Riverfront Plaza
Newark, NJ 07102
(201) 622-5303

Rowena Duran
Hurley & Vasios
636 Morris Tpk.
Short Hills, NJ 07078
(201) 467-1300

Daniel M. Hurley
Hurley & Vasios
636 Morris Tpk.
Short Hills, NJ 07078
(201) 467-1300

Thomas Kelly, Jr.
Hurley & Vasios
636 Morris Tpk.
Short Hills, NJ 07078
(201) 467-1300

James A. Vasios
Hurley & Vasios
636 Morris Tpk.
Short Hills, NJ 07078
(201) 467-1300

Roy J. Konray
Konray & Tonelli, P.C.
242 St. Paul St.
Westfield, NJ 07091-2908
(908) 654-0505

NEW MEXICO

Turner W. Branch
Law Office of Turner W.
    Branch
2025 Rio Grande Blvd. NW
Albuquerque, NM 87104
(505) 243-3501

Roger Eaton
Law Office of Roger Eaton
1776 Montano Rd. NW, Bldg. 2
Albuquerque, NM 87107
(505) 345-1771

Ronald C. Morgan
Law Office of Ronald C.
    Morgan
P.O. Box 25686
Albuquerque, NM 87125-5686
(505) 842-1905

Alexander A. Wold, Jr.
Bell & Associates
610 7th St. NW
Albuquerque, NM 87102
(505) 242-7979

Richard C. Bosson
Bosson & Canepa, P.A.
200 W. De Vargas St.
P.O. Box 1775
Santa Fe, NM 87501-1775
(505) 982-9229

Michael Schwarz
Law Office of Michael Schwarz
P.O. Box 1656
Santa Fe, NM 87504-1656
(505) 988-2053

NEW YORK

Peter Bouman
Coughlin & Gerhart
1 Marine Midland Plaza
Binghamton, NY 13902
(607) 723-9511

Michael Drezin
Law Office of Michael Drezin
25 Westchester Sq.
Bronx, NY 10461
(212) 823-7211

Philip H. Magner, Jr.
Magner, Love & Morris, P.C.
1725 Statler Towers
Buffalo, NY 14202
(716) 856-8480

James E. Morris
Morris, Cantor & Barnes
711 Chemical Bldg.
69 Delaware Ave.
Buffalo, NY 14202
(716) 852-1888

Thomas McElligott
McElligott, Kujawski &
  DelliCarpini
1637 Deer Park Ave.
Deer Park, NY 11729
(516) 667-7272

James Sawyer
Sawyer, Davis & Halpern
200 Garden City Plaza,
  Suite 300
Garden City, NY 11530
(516) 248-4500

Jon C. Dupée
Dupée & Orloff
30 Matthews St.
P.O. Box 470
Goshen, NY 10924-0470
(914) 294-8900

Robert Horowitz
Robert Horowitz, P.C.
488 Great Neck Rd.
Great Neck, NY 11021
(516) 829-8980

Roy M. Warner
5 Dakota Dr., Suite 202
Lake Success, NY 11042
(516) 248-7600

Alan C. Levy
Law Offices of Alan C. Levy
100 Herricks Rd.
Mineola, NY 11501
(516) 741-7300

Raymond W. Belair
Belair & Evans
61 Broadway
New York, NY 10006
(212) 344-3900

Andrew P. Davis
Davis & Davis
116 John St.
New York, NY 10038
(212) 962-1111

Michael B. Gluck
DiJoseph & Gluck
233 Broadway, Suite 4000
New York, NY 10279
(212) 233-3200

Herman M. Goldberg
Law Offices of Herman M.
   Goldberg
275 Madison Ave.
New York, NY 10016
(212) 684-3548

Paul D. Rheingold
Rheingold & McGowan, P.C.
113 E. 37th St.
New York, NY 10016
(212) 684-1880

Alfred P. Kremer
Law Office of Alfred P. Kremer
2 State St., Suite 950
Rochester, NY 14614-1305
(716) 546-6040

Daniel S. Pellegrin
Law Office of Daniel S.
   Pellegrin
19 Court Plaza, Suite 301
White Plains, NY 10601
(914) 428-5252

NORTH CAROLINA

William H. Holdford
Narron, Holdford, Babb,
   Harrison & Rhodes
204 N. Tarboro St.
P.O. Box 279
Wilson, NC 27894-0279
(919) 237-3153

NORTH DAKOTA

James L. Norris
James L. Norris, P.C.
313 N. 1st St.
P.O. Box 978
Bismarck, ND 58502-0978
(701) 255-2301

Frederick E. Saefke, Jr.
Frederick E. Saefke, Jr. Law
   Office
411 N. 4th St.
P.O. Box 1874
Bismarck, ND 58502-1874
(701) 255-1344

William P. Zuger
Zuger Law Offices
2800 N. Washington St.
Bismarck, ND 58501
(701) 255-7572

OHIO

R. David Briggs
Briggs & Pry
1655 W. Market St., Suite 400
Akron, OH 44313
(216) 864-6611

V. Lee Sinclair, Jr.
Amerman, Burt & Jones Co.,
L.P.A.
624 Market Ave. N
Canton, OH 44720
(216) 456-2491

Donald C. Steiner
Steiner Law Office
648 Citizens Savings Bldg.
Canton, OH 44702
(216) 454-8056

Jim Rimedio
Law Office of Jim Rimedio
103 Hosea Ave.
Cincinnati, OH 45220
(513) 977-4211

John E. Rockel
Law Office of John E. Rockel
1 W. 4th St., Suite 2300
Cincinnati, OH 45202
(513) 421-4545

Roger C. Stridsberg
Law Office of Roger C.
Stridsberg
917 Main St., Suite 400
Cincinnati, OH 45202
(513) 977-4211

Julian Cohen
Cohen & Steinberg
1600 Standard Bldg.
Cleveland, OH 44113
(216) 696-1035

Howard D. Mishkind
Weisman, Goldberg, Weisman
& Kaufman Co., L.P.A.
1600 Midland Bldg.
101 Prospect Ave. W
Cleveland, OH 44115
(216) 781-1111

Gerald L. Steinberg
Cohen & Steinberg
1600 Standard Bldg.
Cleveland, OH 44113
(216) 696-1035

Eugene L. Matan
Matan & Smith
261 S. Front St.
Columbus, OH 43215
(614) 228-2678

Dale K. Perdue
Clark, Perdue & Roberts Co.,
L.P.A.
471 E. Broad St., Suite 1601
Columbus, OH 43215
(614) 469-1601

Claudia Turrell
Turrell & Ferguson
120 W. 2nd St.
Dayton, OH 45402
(513) 461-1833

William R. McCarty
Martin, McCarty, Richman &
Wright Co., L.P.A.
26 N. Wright Ave.
Fairborn, OH 45324
(513) 878-8649

Larry L. Inscore
Inscore, Rinehardt, Whitney &
Enderle
3 N. Main St.
Mansfield, OH 44902
(419) 522-2733

OKLAHOMA

Monty L. Bratcher
Monty L. Bratcher, P.C.
2000 S.E. 15th St.
P.O. Box 1347
Edmond, OK 73083-1347
(405) 340-6983

Rex Friend
Parr & Friend
3010 Classen Blvd.
Oklahoma City, OK 73106
(405) 528-1018

John D. Boydston
W. C. "Bill" Sellers, Inc.
P.O. Box 1404
Sapulpa, OK 74067-1404
(918) 224-5357

John L. Harlan
Harlan, Harlan & Branscum,
    P.C.
404 E. Dewey St.
P.O. Box 1326
Sapulpa, OK 74067-1326
(918) 227-2590

James K. Deuschle
Hoel, Deuschle, Shelton & Holt
1518 S. Cheyenne
Tulsa, OK 74117
(918) 592-2275

Michael J. Fairchild
Law Office of Michael J.
    Fairchild
The Downing Mansion
232 N. Santa Fe
Tulsa, OK 74127
(918) 585-1544

OREGON

Gary M. Berne
Stoll, Stoll, Berne & Lokting,
    P.C.
209 S.W. Oak St.
Portland, OR 97225
(503) 227-1600

Jeffrey A. Bowersox
Williams, Troutwine &
    Bowersox, P.C.
1100 S.W. 6th Ave., Suite 1100
Portland, OR 97204
(503) 295-2924

Jeffrey P. Foote
Law Offices of Jeffrey P. Foote
1020 S.W. Taylor St., Suite 800
Portland, OR 97205
(503) 228-1133

Michael A. Greene
Rosenthal & Greene, P.C.
1907 1001 S.W. 5th Ave.
Portland, OR 97204
(503) 228-3015

Charles J. Merten
Merten & Associates
720 S.W. Washington St.,
    Suite 311
Portland, OR 97205
(503) 227-3157

Michael R. Shinn
Law Office of Michael R. Shinn
219 S.W. Stark St.
Portland, OR 97204
(503) 242-0113

Michael L. Williams
Williams, Troutwine &
  Bowersox, P.C.
1100 S.W. 6th Ave., Suite 1100
Portland, OR 97204-1094
(503) 295-2924

D. Lawrence Wobbrock
Law Office of D. Lawrence
  Wobbrock
1020 S.W. Taylor St., Suite 800
Portland, OR 97205
(503) 228-6600

PENNSYLVANIA

John R. Wingerter
Carney & Good
254 W. 6th St.
Erie, PA 16507
(814) 453-5004

Richard C. Angino
Angino & Rovner, P.C.
4503 N. Front St.
Harrisburg, PA 17110
(717) 238-6791

Marvin Beshore
Milspaw & Beshore
126 Locust St.
P.O. Box 946
Harrisburg, PA 17108-0946
(717) 236-0781

Christopher S. Underhill
Hartman, Underhill &
  Brubaker
221 E. Chestnut St.
Lancaster, PA 17602
(717) 299-7254

Gary Brownstein
Gary Brownstein, P.C.
1308 Spruce St.
Philadelphia, PA 19107
(215) 732-4780

Mark R. Cuker
Williams & Cuker
1650 Arch St., Suite 2350
Philadelphia, PA 19103
(215) 557-0099

Andrew DiPiero
Rutter, Turner, Solomon &
  DiPiero
The Curtis Center, Suite 750
Independence Sq. W
Philadelphia, PA 19106
(215) 925-9200

Gary Green
Sidkoff, Pincus & Green, P.C.
530 Walnut St., 12th Floor
Philadelphia, PA 19106
(215) 574-0600

Thomas B. Rutter
Rutter, Turner, Solomon &
  DiPiero
The Curtis Center, Suite 750
Independence Sq. W
Philadelphia, PA 19106
(215) 925-9200

Gregory L. Schell
Rutter, Turner, Solomon &
  DiPiero
The Curtis Center, Suite 750
Independence Sq. W
Philadelphia, PA 19106
(215) 925-9200

Andrew A. Solomon
Rutter, Turner, Solomon &
  DiPiero
The Curtis Center, Suite 750
Independence Sq. W
Philadelphia, PA 19106
(215) 925-9200

John M. Willis
Bernstein, Bernstein &
  Harrison
1600 Market St., Suite 2500
Philadelphia, PA 19103
(215) 864-0770

Paul M. Goltz
Law Office of Paul M. Goltz
810 Allegheny Bldg.
429 Forbes Ave.
Pittsburgh, PA 15219
(412) 281-0846

John P. Lydon
Sikov & Love, P.A.
1400 Lawyers Bldg.
Pittsburgh, PA 15227
(412) 261-4202

Samuel C. Stretton
Law Office of Samuel C.
  Stretton
301 S. High St.
P.O. Box 3231
West Chester, PA 19381-3231
(215) 696-4243

RHODE ISLAND

Richard A. Boren
Licht & Semonoff
1 Park Row
Providence, RI 02903
(401) 421-8030

SOUTH CAROLINA

A. Camden Lewis
Lewis, Babcock, Pleicones &
  Hawkins
P.O. Box 11280
Columbia, SC 29211-1280
(803) 771-8000

Cheryl F. Perkins
Perkins Law Firm
1103 Beaufort St.
Columbia, SC 29201
(803) 771-1554

SOUTH DAKOTA

Rick Johnson
Johnson, Eklund & Davis
P.O. Box 149
Gregory, SD 57533-0149
(605) 835-8391

TENNESSEE

Charles P. Dupree
Law Office of Charles P.
  Dupree
6400 Lee Hwy., Suite 104
Chattanooga, TN 37421
(615) 855-1841

T. Robert Hill
Hill, Boren, Drew &
  Martindale, P.C.
1269 N. Highland Ave.
Jackson, TN 38301
(901) 423-3300

William Vines
Butler, Vines, Babb &
  Threadgill
1st American Bank Center,
  8th Floor
Knoxville, TN 37902
(615) 637-3531

James M. Glasgow
Elam, Glasgow & Acree
Sovran Bank Bldg.
127 S. 1st St.
Union City, TN 38261
(901) 885-2011

TEXAS

Michael G. Burk
Burk & Watt
1102 W. 6th St.
Austin, TX 78703
(512) 473-2722

Gary F. DeShazo
Gary F. DeShazo & Associates
114 W. 7th St., Suite 1200
Austin, TX 78701
(512) 476-3800

Dicky Grigg
Spivey, Grigg, Kelly & Knisely
48 East Ave.
Austin, TX 78701
(512) 474-6061

Thomas R. Harkness
Whitehurst, Harkness &
  Watson
P.O. Box 1802
Austin, TX 78767-1802
(512) 476-4346

Pat Kelly
Spivey, Grigg, Kelly & Knisely
48 East Ave.
Austin, TX 78701
(512) 474-6061

Paul E. Knisely
Spivey, Grigg, Kelly & Knisely
48 East Ave.
Austin, TX 78701
(512) 474-6061

Broadus A. Spivey
Spivey, Grigg, Kelly & Knisely
48 East Ave.
Austin, TX 78701
(512) 474-6061

Michael A. Wash
Law Office of Michael A. Wash
221 W. 6th St., Suite 810
Austin, TX 78701
(512) 480-9494

Robert L. Tobey
Johnson & Budner, P.C.
1445 Ross Ave., Suite 3700
Dallas, TX 75202
(214) 855-6260

Jim L. Culpepper
Culpepper, Cox & Bryant
952 Echo Lane, Suite 424
Houston, TX 77084
(713) 932-9907

Larry J. Doherty
Doherty, Norman &
  Williamson
2225 La Branch St.
Houston, TX 77002
(713) 652-5711

Beaumont Martin
Law Offices of David Lam
7322 S.W. Freeway, Suite 460
Houston, TX 77074
(713) 772-7088

Glen E. Beaman
Law Office of Glen E. Beaman
P.O. Box 6449
Kingwood, TX 77325-6449
(800) 622-3440

Gerald K. Fugit
Law Office of Gerald K. Fugit
412 N. Texas
Odessa, TX 79761-5198
(915) 332-1661

Franklin D. Houser
Tinsman & Houser, Inc.
1400 1 Riverwalk Pl.
San Antonio, TX 78205
(512) 225-3121

UTAH

Barbara K. Polich
Parsons, Behle & Latimer
P.O. Box 11898
Salt Lake City, UT 84105-1898
(801) 532-1234

David E. West
Armstrong, Rawlings & West
1300 Walker Center
175 S. Main
Salt Lake City, UT 84111
(801) 359-2093

VERMONT

Frederick deG. Harlow
Harlow, Liccardi & Crawford,
    P.C.
92 Center St.
Rutland, VT 05701
(802) 775-3368

Herbert G. Ogden, Jr.
Harlow, Liccardi & Crawford,
    P.C.
92 Center St.
Rutland, VT 05701
(802) 775-3368

VIRGINIA

John C. Lowe
John C. Lowe, P.C.
300 Court Sq.
Charlottesville, VA 22901
(804) 296-8188

Roger G. Nord
Law Office of Roger G. Nord
10627 Jones St.
Fairfax, VA 22030
(703) 273-4010

Steven M. Garver
Garver & Moller
11707 Bowman Green Dr.
P.O. Box 2430
Reston, VA 22090-2430
(703) 471-1090

Thomas B. Shuttleworth
Shuttleworth, Ruloff, Giordano
    & Kahle
4425 Corporation Lane,
    Suite 30
Virginia Beach, VA 23462
(804) 671-6000

WASHINGTON

John A. Hoglund
Law Office of John A. Hoglund
4th & Capitol Way
Olympia, WA 98507
(206) 786-1717

A. Stephen Anderson
A. Stephen Anderson, P.C.
520 E. Denny Way
Seattle, WA 98122
(206) 325-2801

James E. Baker
Miracle, Pruzan & Pruzan
1000 2nd Ave., Suite 1550
Seattle, WA 98104
(206) 624-8830

David J. Balint
De Funis & Balint, P.S.
2033 6th Ave., Suite 800
Seattle, WA 98121
(206) 728-7799

Robert B. Gould
Law Offices of Robert B. Gould
2121 4th Ave., Suite 320
Seattle, WA 98121
(206) 441-4440

W. Ronald Groshong
Groshong, Lehet & Thornton
2133 3rd Ave.
Seattle, WA 98121-2325
(206) 448-7172

Roger M. Leed
Roger M. Leed, P.S.
1001 4th Ave., Suite 4301
Seattle, WA 98154
(206) 382-0217

David Middaugh
Law Office of David Middaugh
600 1st Ave., Suite 408
Seattle, WA 98104
(206) 682-5615

Christopher C. Pence
Pence & Dawson
509 2nd Ave., Suite 3000
Seattle, WA 98104
(206) 624-5000

George A. Thornton
Groshong, Lehet & Thornton
2133 3rd Ave.
Seattle, WA 98121-2325
(206) 448-7172

John L. Messina
Messina & Duffy
4002 Tacoma Mall Blvd.,
   Suite 200
Tacoma, WA 98409
(206) 472-6000

WEST VIRGINIA

Bruce L. Freeman
Hunt & Wilson
7 Players Club Dr.
Charleston, WV 25311
(304) 344-9651

James B. Lees, Jr.
Hunt & Wilson
7 Players Club Dr.
Charleston, WV 25311
(304) 344-9651

Robert D. Aitcheson
Robert D. Aitcheson, L.C.
206-8 N. George St.
P.O. Box 750
Charles Town, WV 25414-0750
(304) 725-2002

WISCONSIN

Edward P. Rudolph
Rudolph & Rudolph
700 Pilgrim Pkwy.
Elm Grove, WI 53122
(414) 782-7887

Richard A. Boltz
Boltz & Whetter
425 S. Adams St.
Green Bay, WI 54301
(414) 432-5551

Lee R. Atterbury
Atterbury, Riley, Luebke &
    Pretto, S.C.
411 W. Main St.
Madison, WI 53703
(608) 257-4715

Brian E. Butler
Stafford, Rosenbaum, Rieser &
    Hansen
3 S. Pickney St., Suite 1000
Madison, WI 53703
(608) 256-0226

Robert A. Pretto
Atterbury, Riley, Luebke &
    Pretto, S.C.
411 W. Main St.
Madison, WI 53703
(608) 257-4715

Phillip M. Steans,
Steans, Skinner, Schofield &
    Higley
2403 Stout Rd.
Menomonie, WI 54751
(715) 235-9631

Gordon K. Aaron
Axel, Aaron & Goldman
161 W. Wisconsin Ave.,
    Suite 6174
Milwaukee, WI 53209
(414) 273-6300

William M. Cannon
Cannon & Dunphy
1110 N. Old World 3rd St.,
    Suite 600
Milwaukee, WI 53203
(414) 276-0111

John H. Correll
Correll Law Office
710 N. Plankinton Ave.
Milwaukee, WI 53203
(414) 271-7979

Patrick O. Dunphy
Cannon & Dunphy
1110 N. Old World 3rd St.,
    Suite 600
Milwaukee, WI 53203
(414) 276-0111

Irving D. Gaines
Gaines Law Offices, S.C.
312 E. Wisconsin Ave.,
    Suite 208
Milwaukee, WI 53202
(414) 271-1938

Lynn R. Laufenberg
Cannon & Dunphy
1110 N. Old World 3rd St.,
    Suite 600
Milwaukee, WI 53203
(414) 276-0111

James C. Reiher
Von Briesen & Purtell, S.C.
411 E. Wisconsin Ave.,
    Suite 700
Milwaukee, WI 53202
(414) 276-1122

Ray E. Schrank
Cannon & Dunphy
1110 N. Old World 3rd St.,
    Suite 600
Milwaukee, WI 53203
(414) 276-0111

Robert A. Slattery
Slattery & Hausman, Ltd.
111 E. Kilbourn Ave.
Milwaukee, WI 53202
(414) 271-4555

Mark L. Thomsen
Cannon & Dunphy
1110 N. Old World 3rd St.,
    Suite 600
Milwaukee, WI 53203
(414) 276-0111

Ronald M. Wawrzyn
Foley & Lardner
777 E. Wisconsin Ave.,
    Suite 3900
Milwaukee, WI 53202
(414) 289-3554

John E. Danner
Harrold, Scrobell & Danner,
    S.C.
315 Oneida St.
P.O. Box 1148
Minocqua, WI 54548-1148
(715) 356-9591

Gregory J. Harrold
Harrold, Scrobell & Danner,
    S.C.
315 Oneida St.
P.O. Box 1148
Minocqua, WI 54548-1148
(715) 356-9591

WYOMING

Michael M. Hoch
Michael M. Hoch & Associates
410 Grand St., Suite 105
Laramie, WY 82070
(307) 742-4755

HOW THE DISCIPLINARY PROCESS WORKS

Although each state's grievance system operates independently, almost all follow the model described below, with slight variations.

In almost every state, the highest court has oversight of attorney discipline. Actual court control, however, is nominal in most states and usually involves little more than rubber-stamping disciplinary agency decisions.

The ABA reports that in thirty-three states the agencies are run by state bar associations. In these, as in other states, the bar also acts as a trade association, charged with protecting the status and economic interests of the legal profession. In the remaining states, although the disciplinary agency is technically independent of the state bar, the state bar has considerable influence over who sits on the agency's governing board, who is hired as bar counsel (the agency director, traditionally a lawyer), how complaints are processed and what is considered unethical conduct under the state's code of professional responsibility.

The disciplinary process begins when someone files a complaint with the bar counsel. Complaints can be initiated by clients, judges, other lawyers or the disciplinary agency itself. Lawyers and judges are required by their codes of ethics to report unethical or incompetent conduct by lawyers. Nevertheless, almost all complaints are filed by clients.

Complaints are screened by the bar counsel's staff to determine whether they allege misconduct under the state's code. Many complaints do not survive this initial screening, but there is very little information about dismissals at the screening stage because almost no agencies allow the public access to these records.

Only complaints that survive initial screening are investigated. The investigation almost always includes asking the lawyer named in the complaint to respond to the client's claims. Investigations can—but often do not—include gathering documents and conducting interviews. If the bar counsel determines that it is more likely than not that the lawyer has violated the ethical code (finds "probable cause"), a panel is appointed to hear the complaint. Only about one of every twelve complaints reaches this stage.

The hearing panel usually has three members, most often three lawyers or two lawyers and one nonlawyer. Rules of procedure typically apply during hearings, and the lawyer, though not under obligation to defend questionable conduct, is given many of the due-process rights afforded criminal defendants. For discipline to be imposed, misconduct must be proven, in most states by evidence that meets the tough "clear and convincing" standard.

After the hearing, the panel reports its findings and recommendation to the agency's governing board, which then reviews the recommendation and decides whether to uphold it. Usually, the board can dismiss the complaint, issue a private reprimand or recommend public discipline to the court. If a formal charge recommending public discipline is filed with the court, the court often appoints a referee to review the recommendation. In some states the referee holds a hearing, during which the bar counsel presents evidence supporting the agency's recommendation, and the lawyer has an opportunity to present a defense.

Based on the referee's findings, the court can dismiss the complaint or impose discipline. Typical options for discipline include a public reprimand, a suspension of the law-

After a Complaint Is Filed

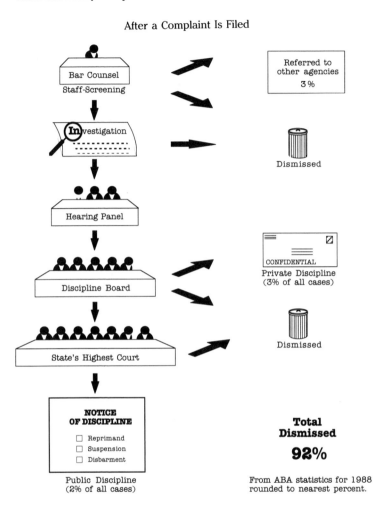

Bar Counsel
Staff-Screening

Referred to
other agencies
3%

Investigation

Dismissed

Hearing Panel

Discipline Board

CONFIDENTIAL
Private Discipline
(3% of all cases)

Dismissed

State's Highest Court

**NOTICE
OF DISCIPLINE**

☐ Reprimand
☐ Suspension
☐ Disbarment

Public Discipline
(2% of all cases)

**Total
Dismissed**

92%

From ABA statistics for 1988
rounded to nearest percent.

yer's license to practice for a specified period, and disbarment. Disbarred lawyers lose their license to practice law, although they may usually reapply for a license after five years. In most states, the lawyer has the right to appeal the court's decision; in almost all states, the agency may appeal; and in some states, the client may appeal.

STATE BAR PROGRAMS FOR RESOLVING COMPLAINTS AGAINST LAWYERS

This appendix lists addresses and phone numbers for grievance committees, client security trust fund offices and fee arbitration programs for all fifty states, the District of Columbia, the Virgin Islands and Puerto Rico.

Where state offices handle the matter, that office is listed. If the issue is handled at a local office, either that office is listed or we suggest that you contact the state office for a local referral.

All information is accurate as of February 1991. Data on grievance committees and client security trust fund offices were compiled by the American Bar Association, and the fee arbitration program data were compiled by HALT. Because the names and addresses of state agencies may change at any time, you should verify the information with your state bar or the American Bar Association.

ALABAMA

Attorney Grievance
State Office:
General Counsel
Alabama State Bar
Center for Professional
    Responsibility
1019 S. Perry St.
Montgomery, AL 36104
(205) 269-1515

Client Security Trust Fund
Executive Director
Alabama State Bar
P.O. Box 671
415 Dexter St.
Montgomery, AL 36101
(205) 269-1515

Fee Arbitration
No statewide program; state
  bar refers cases to local fee
  arbitration where available.
(Address, telephone same as
  for Client Security Trust
  Fund.)

ALASKA
Attorney Grievance
State Office:
Bar Counsel
Alaska Bar Association
P.O. Box 100279
Anchorage, AK 99510
(907) 272-7469

Client Security Trust Fund
Assistant Bar Counsel
(Address, telephone same as
  for Attorney Grievance.)

Fee Arbitration
Fee Arbitration Committee
(Address, telephone same as
  for Attorney Grievance.)

ARIZONA
Attorney Grievance
State Office:
Chief Bar Counsel
State Bar of Arizona
363 N. First Ave.
Phoenix, AZ 85003-1580
(602) 252-4804

Client Security Trust Fund
Chief Bar Counsel
(Address, telephone same as
  for Attorney Grievance.)

Fee Arbitration
Committee on Arbitration of
  Fee Disputes
(Address, telephone same as
  for Attorney Grievance.)

ARKANSAS
Attorney Grievance
State Office:
Supreme Court of Arkansas
Committee on Professional
  Conduct
364 Prospect Bldg.
1501 N. University
Little Rock, AR 72207
(501) 664-8658

Client Security Trust Fund
Clerk
Arkansas Supreme Court
  Justice Bldg.
625 Marshall St.
Little Rock, AR 72201
(501) 682-6849

Fee Arbitration
None.

CALIFORNIA
Attorney Grievance
Chief Trial Counsel
Intake/Legal Advice
State Bar of California
333 S. Beaudry Ave., 9th Floor
Los Angeles, CA 90017
(213) 580-5000
(800) 843-9053 (California
  residents only)

Client Security Trust Fund
(Address same as for Attorney
   Grievance.)
(213) 580-5140
(800) 843-9053 (California
   residents only)

Fee Arbitration
State Bar of California
Mandatory Fee Arbitration
100 Van Ness Ave., 28th Floor
San Francisco, CA 94102-5238
(415) 241-2020

COLORADO
Attorney Grievance
State Office:
Disciplinary Counsel
Supreme Court of Colorado
600 17th St., Suite 510 S.
Dominion Plaza Bldg.
Denver, CO 80202
(303) 893-8121

Client Security Trust Fund
Executive Director
Colorado Bar Association
1900 Grant St., Suite 950
Denver, CO 80203-4309
(303) 860-1112

Fee Arbitration
Legal Fee Arbitration
   Committee
(Address, telephone same as
   for Client Security Trust
   Fund.)

CONNECTICUT
Attorney Grievance
State Office:
Statewide Bar Counsel
P.O. Box 260888, Station A
Hartford, CT 06126-0888
(203) 566-4163

Client Security Trust Fund
Asst. Executive Director
Connecticut Bar Association
101 Corporate Place
Rocky Hill, CT 06067
(203) 721-0025

Fee Arbitration
Committee on Arbitration of
   Fee Disputes
(Address, telephone same as
   for Client Security Trust
   Fund.)

DELAWARE
Attorney Grievance
State Office:
Disciplinary Counsel
Board on Professional
   Responsibility of the
   Supreme Court of Delaware
831 Tatnall St.
P.O. Box 1808
Wilmington, DE 19899
(302) 571-8703

Client Security Trust Fund
Administrator
Delaware State Bar Association
708 Market St.
P.O. Box 1709
Wilmington, DE 19899
(302) 658-5278

Fee Arbitration
Fee Dispute Conciliation and
  Mediation Committee
(Address, telephone same as
  for Client Security Trust
  Fund.)

DISTRICT OF COLUMBIA

Attorney Grievance
District Office:
Bar Counsel
District of Columbia Bar
Bldg. A, Room 127
515 5th St. NW
Washington, DC 20001
(202) 638-1501

Client Security Trust Fund
Assistant Executive Director
District of Columbia Bar
1707 L St. NW, 6th Floor
Washington, DC 20036
(202) 331-3883

Fee Arbitration
Attorney-Client Arbitration
  Board
(Address, telephone same as
  for Client Security Trust
  Fund.)

FLORIDA

Attorney Grievance
State Office:
Staff Counsel
Florida Bar
650 Apalachee Pkwy.
Tallahassee, FL 32399-2300
(800) 874-0005 (out of state)
(800) 342-8060 (Florida
  residents only)
(904) 561-5839

Client Security Trust Fund
Programs Division
(Address same as for Attorney
  Grievance.)
(904) 561-5600

Fee Arbitration
Fee Arbitration Committee
(Address, telephone same as
  for Attorney Grievance.)

GEORGIA

Attorney Grievance
State Office:
General Counsel
State Bar of Georgia
50 Hurt Plaza, Suite 800
Atlanta, GA 30303
(404) 527-8720

Client Security Trust Fund
Assistant General Counsel
(Address, telephone same as
  for Attorney Grievance.)

Fee Arbitration
Committee on Arbitration of
  Fee Disputes
(Address same as for Attorney
  Grievance.)
(404) 527-8750

HAWAII

Attorney Grievance
State Office:
Chief Disciplinary Counsel
Office of Disciplinary Counsel
Supreme Court of the State of
  Hawaii
1164 Bishop St., Suite 600
Honolulu, HI 96813
(808) 521-4591

Client Security Trust Fund
Fund Administrator
Grosvenor Center
737 Bishop St., Suite 1820
Honolulu, HI 96813
(808) 599-8938

Fee Arbitration
Attorney-Client Coordination
  Committee
Hawaii State Bar Association
P.O. Box 26
Honolulu, HI 96810
(808) 537-1868

IDAHO

Attorney Grievance
State Office:
Bar Counsel
Idaho State Bar
P.O. Box 895
204 W. State St.
Boise, ID 83701
(208) 342-8958

Client Security Trust Fund
Executive Director
(Address, telephone same as
  for Attorney Grievance.)

Fee Arbitration
Fee Arbitration Program
(Address, telephone same as
  for Attorney Grievance.)

ILLINOIS

Attorney Grievance
Chicago and Northern Illinois:
Attorney Registration &
  Disciplinary Commission of
  the Supreme Court of
  Illinois
203 N. Wabash Ave.,
  Suite 1900
Chicago, IL 60601-2474
(312) 346-0690
(800) 826-8625 (Illinois
  residents only)

Central and Southern Illinois:
Attorney Registration &
  Disciplinary Commission of
  the Supreme Court of
  Illinois
One N. Old Capitol Plaza,
  Suite 330
Springfield, IL 62701-1507
(217) 522-6838
(800) 252-8048 (Illinois
  residents only)

Client Security Trust Fund
Clients' Security Fund of the
  Bar of Illinois
Illinois Bar Center
Springfield, IL 62701
(217) 525-1760

Fee Arbitration
Voluntary Fee Arbitration
(Address, telephone same as
  for Client Security Trust
  Fund.)

INDIANA

Attorney Grievance
State Office:
Executive Secretary
Disciplinary Commission of
   the Supreme Court of
   Indiana
628 I.S.T.A. Bldg., Room 814
150 W. Market St.
Indianapolis, IN 46204
(317) 232-1807

Client Security Trust Fund
Executive Director
Indiana Bar Center
Indiana State Bar Association
230 E. Ohio St.,
Indianapolis, IN 46204
(317) 639-5465

Fee Arbitration
No statewide program; state
   bar refers cases to local fee
   arbitration where available.
(Address, telephone same as
   for Client Security Trust
   Fund.)

IOWA

Attorney Grievance
State Office:
Ethics Administrator
Iowa State Bar Association
1101 Fleming Bldg.
Des Moines, IA 50309
(515) 243-3179

Client Security Trust Fund
Assistant Court Administrator
Clients' Security Trust Fund
State Capitol
Des Moines, IA 50319
(515) 246-8076

Fee Arbitration
No statewide program; state
   bar refers cases to local fee
   arbitration where available.
(Address, telephone same as
   for Attorney Grievance.)

KANSAS

Attorney Grievance
State Office:
Disciplinary Administrator
Supreme Court of Kansas
Kansas Judicial Center, Room
   278
301 W. 10th St.
Topeka, KS 66612
(913) 296-2486

Client Security Trust Fund
None.

Fee Arbitration
No statewide program; state
   bar refers cases to local fee
   arbitration where available.
(Address, telephone same as
   for Attorney Grievance.)

KENTUCKY

Attorney Grievance
State Office:
Bar Counsel
Kentucky Bar Association
W. Main at Kentucky River
Frankfort, KY 40601
(502) 564-3795

Client Security Trust Fund
(Address, telephone same as
   for Attorney Grievance.)

Fee Arbitration
Legal Fee Arbitration Plan
(Address, telephone same as
  for Attorney Grievance.)

LOUISIANA
Attorney Grievance
State Office:
Chief Disciplinary Counsel
Disciplinary Board
Louisiana State Bar
  Association
601 St. Charles Ave., 4th Floor
New Orleans, LA 70130
(504) 523-1414

Client Security Trust Fund
Executive Counsel
(Address, telephone same as
  for Attorney Grievance.)

Fee Arbitration
None.

MAINE
Attorney Grievance
State Office:
Bar Counsel
Maine Board of Overseers of
  the Bar
P.O. Box 1820
Augusta, ME 04332-1820
(207) 623-1121

Client Security Trust Fund
None.

Fee Arbitration
Fee Arbitration Commission
(Address, telephone same as
  for Attorney Grievance.)

MARYLAND
Attorney Grievance
State Office:
Bar Counsel
Attorney Grievance
  Commission of Maryland
District Court Bldg.
580 Taylor Ave., Room 404
Annapolis, MD 21401
(301) 974-2791

Client Security Trust Fund
Administrator
Box 284
18222 Flower Hill Way
Gaithersburg, MD 20879
(301) 990-8812

Fee Arbitration
Committee on Resolution of
  Fee Disputes
(Address, telephone same as
  for Client Security Trust
  Fund.)

MASSACHUSETTS
Attorney Grievance
State Office:
Bar Counsel
Massachusetts Board of Bar
  Overseers
11 Beacon St.
Boston, MA 02108
(617) 357-1860

Client Security Trust Fund
Assistant Board Counsel
75 Federal St.
Boston, MA 02110
(617) 357-1860

Fee Arbitration
Fee Arbitration Board
Massachusetts Bar Association
20 West St.
Boston, MA 02111
(617) 542-3602

MICHIGAN
Attorney Grievance
State Office:
Acting Grievance
  Administrator
Michigan Attorney Grievance
  Commission
Marquette Bldg., Suite 256
243 W. Congress
Detroit, MI 48226
(313) 961-6585

Client Security Trust Fund
State Bar of Michigan
306 Townsend St.
Lansing, MI 48933-2083
(517) 372-9030, ext. 3010

Fee Arbitration
Fee Arbitration Program
(Address, telephone same as
  for Attorney Grievance.)

MINNESOTA
Attorney Grievance
State Office:
Director
Office of Lawyers' Professional
  Responsibility
520 Lafayette Rd., 1st Floor
St. Paul, MN 55155-4196
(612) 296-3952
(800) 657-3601 (Minnesota
  residents only)

Client Security Trust Fund
Director
(Address, telephone same as
  for Attorney Grievance.)

Fee Arbitration
No statewide program;
  disciplinary committee
  refers cases to local fee
  arbitration where available.
(Address, telephone same as
  for Attorney Grievance.)

MISSISSIPPI
Attorney Grievance
State Office:
General Counsel
Mississippi State Bar
643 N. State St.
P.O. Box 2168
Jackson, MS 39225-2168
(601) 948-4471

Client Security Trust Fund
Assistant General Counsel
(Address, telephone same as
  for Attorney Grievance.)

Fee Arbitration
Resolution of Fee Disputes
  Committee
(Address, telephone same as
  for Attorney Grievance.)

MISSOURI
Attorney Grievance
State Office:
General Chair
Missouri Bar Administration
P.O. Box 349
Sedalia, MO 65302-0349
(816) 826-7890

Client Security Trust Fund
Director of Programs
Missouri Bar
P.O. Box 119
Jefferson City, MO 65102
(314) 635-4128

Fee Arbitration
No statewide program; state
    bar refers cases to local fee
    arbitration where available.
(Address, telephone same as
    for Attorney Grievance.)

MONTANA
Attorney Grievance
State Office:
Administrative Secretary
Commission on Practice of the
    Supreme Court of Montana
Justice Bldg., Room 315
215 N. Sanders
Helena, MT 59620
(406) 444-2608

Client Security Trust Fund
Executive Director
State Bar of Montana
P.O. Box 577
Helena, MT 59624
(406) 442-7660

Fee Arbitration
Voluntary Fee Arbitration
(Address, telephone same as
    for Client Security Trust
    Fund.)

NEBRASKA
Attorney Grievance
State Office:
Counsel for Discipline
Nebraska State Bar Association
P.O. Box 81809
Lincoln, NE 68501
(402) 475-7091

Client Security Trust Fund
Executive Director
Nebraska State Bar Association
635 S. 14th St.
Lincoln, NE 68508
(402) 475-7091

Fee Arbitration
None.

NEVADA
Attorney Grievance
State Office:
Bar Counsel
State Bar of Nevada
500 S. 3rd St., Suite 2
Las Vegas, NV 89101
(702) 382-0502

Client Security Trust Fund
Staff Administrator
State Bar of Nevada
295 Holcomb Ave., Suite 2
Reno, NV 89502
(702) 382-0502

Fee Arbitration
Voluntary Fee Arbitration
    Program
(Address, telephone same as
    for Attorney Grievance.)

NEW HAMPSHIRE

Attorney Grievance
State Office:
Administrator
New Hampshire Supreme
　Court
Professional Conduct
　Committee
18 N. Main St., Suite 205
Concord, NH 03301
(603) 224-5828

Client Security Trust Fund
Staff Liaison
Clients' Indemnity Fund
New Hampshire Bar
　Association
112 Pleasant St.
Concord, NH 03301
(603) 224-6942

Fee Arbitration
Fee Dispute Resolution
　Committee
(Address, telephone same as
　for Client Security Fund.)

NEW JERSEY

Attorney Grievance
State Office:
Director, Office of Attorney
　Ethics
Supreme Court of New Jersey
Richard J. Hughes Justice
　Complex, CN-963
Trenton, NJ 08625
(609) 292-8750

Client Security Trust Fund
Director and Counsel
(Address same as for Attorney
　Grievance, except room
　number is CN-961)
(609) 984-7179

Fee Arbitration
District Fee Arbitration
　Committee
(Address, telephone same as
　for Attorney Grievance.)

NEW MEXICO

Attorney Grievance
State Office:
Chief Disciplinary Counsel
Disciplinary Board of the
　Supreme Court of New
　Mexico
400 Gold SW, Suite 712
Albuquerque, NM 87102
(505) 842-5781

Client Security Trust Fund
None.

Fee Arbitration
Fee Arbitration Committee
State Bar of New Mexico
P.O. Box 25883
Albuquerque, NM 87125
(505) 842-6132

NEW YORK

Attorney Grievance
*New York City (First Dept.:
　Bronx County):*
Chief Counsel
Departmental Disciplinary
　Committee for the First
　Judicial Department
41 Madison Ave., 39th Floor
New York, NY 10010
(212) 685-1000

*New York City (Second Dept.:
Kings, Queens, Richmond
Counties):*
Chief Counsel
State of New York Grievance
    Committee for the 2nd and
    11th Judicial Districts
Municipal Bldg., 12th Floor
210 Joralemon St.
Brooklyn, NY 11201
(718) 624-7851

*New York State (Second Dept.:
Dutchess, Orange, Putnam,
Rockland, Westchester
Counties):*
Chief Counsel
Grievance Committee for the
    9th Judicial District
Crosswest Office Center
399 Knollwood Rd., Suite 200
White Plains, NY 10603
(914) 949-4540

*New York State (Second Dept.:
Nassau, Suffolk Counties):*
Chief Counsel
New York State Grievance
    Committee for the 10th
    Judicial District
900 Ellison Ave., Room 304
Westbury, NY 11590
(516) 832-8585

*New York State (Third Dept.:
Albany, Broome, Chemung,
Chenango, Clinton,
Columbia, Cortland,
Delaware, Essex, Franklin,
Fulton, Greene, Hamilton,
Madison, Montgomery,
Otsego, Rensselaer, St.
Lawrence, Saratoga,
Schenectady, Schoharie,
Schuyler, Sullivan, Tioga,
Tompkins, Ulster, Warren,
Washington Counties):*
Chief Attorney
3rd Department Committee on
    Professional Standards
Alfred E. Smith State Office
    Bldg., 22nd Floor
P.O. Box 7013, Capitol Station
    Annex
Albany, NY 12225-0013
(518) 474-8816

*New York State (Fourth Dept.:
Herkimer, Jefferson, Lewis,
Oneida, Onondaga, Oswego
Counties):*
Chief Attorney
Appellate Division, Supreme
    Court
4th Judicial Department
Office of Grievance Committee
1036 Ellicott Square Bldg.
Buffalo, NY 14203
(716) 855-1191

Client Security Trust Fund
Executive Director and
    Counsel
Lawyers' Fund for Client
    Protection
55 Elk St.
Albany, NY 12210
(518) 474-8438

Fee Arbitration
No statewide program; state
    bar refers cases to local fee
    arbitration where available.
New York State Bar
1 Elk St.
Albany, NY 12207
(518) 463-3200

NORTH CAROLINA
Attorney Grievance
State Office:
Counsel
North Carolina State Bar
208 Fayetteville St. Mall
P.O. Box 25908
Raleigh, NC 27611
(919) 828-4620

Client Security Trust Fund
Executive Director
(Address, telephone same as
    for Attorney Grievance.)

Fee Arbitration
No statewide program, state
    bar refers cases to local fee
    arbitration where available.
(Address, telephone same as
    for Attorney Grievance.)

NORTH DAKOTA
Attorney Grievance
State Office:
Disciplinary Counsel
Disciplinary Board of the
    Supreme Court
P.O. Box 2297
Bismarck, ND 58502
(701) 224-3348

Client Security Trust Fund
Staff Administrator
State Bar Association of North
    Dakota
P.O. Box 2136
Bismarck, ND 58502
(701) 255-1404

Fee Arbitration
Fee Arbitration Committee
(Address, telephone same as
    for Client Security Trust
    Fund.)

OHIO
Attorney Grievance
State Office:
Disciplinary Counsel
Office of Disciplinary Counsel
    of the Supreme Court of
    Ohio
175 S. 3rd St., Suite 280
Columbus, OH 43215
(614) 461-0256

Summit County:
Executive Director
Akron Bar Association
90 S. High St.
Akron, OH 44308
(216) 253-5007

Hamilton County:
Bar Counsel
Cincinnati Bar Association
35 E. 7th St., Suite 800
Cincinnati, OH 45202-2411
(513) 381-8213

Cuyahoga County:
Counsel
Cleveland Bar Association
113 St. Clair Ave. NE,
    2nd Floor
Cleveland, OH 44114-1253
(216) 696-3525

Franklin County:
Bar Counsel
Columbus Bar Association
175 S. 3rd St.
Columbus, OH 43215-5193
(614) 225-6053

Montgomery County:
Executive Director
Dayton Bar Association
1700 Hulman Bldg.
Dayton, OH 45402-1671
(513) 222-7902

Lucas County:
Executive Director
Toledo Bar Association
311 N. Superior St.
Toledo, OH 43604
(419) 242-9363

Client Security Trust Fund
Supreme Court of Ohio
Clients' Security Trust Fund
175 S. 3rd St., Suite 285
Columbus, OH 43215
(614) 221-0562

Fee Arbitration
No statewide program; state
    bar refers cases to local fee
    arbitration where available.
Ohio State Bar Association
33 W. 11th Ave.
Columbus, OH 43201-2099
(614) 421-2121

OKLAHOMA
Attorney Grievance
State Office:
General Counsel
Oklahoma Bar Center
1901 N. Lincoln Blvd.
P.O. Box 53036
Oklahoma City, OK 73152
(405) 524-2365

Client Security Trust Fund
Executive Director
(Address, telephone same as
    for Attorney Grievance.)

Fee Arbitration
No statewide program; state
    bar refers cases to local fee
    arbitration where available.
(Address, telephone same as
    for Attorney Grievance.)

OREGON
Attorney Grievance
State Office:
Disciplinary Counsel
Oregon State Bar
P.O. Box 1689
Lake Oswego, OR 97035-0889
(503) 620-0222

Client Security Trust Fund
Staff Liaison
Oregon State Bar
5200 S.W. Meadows Rd.
P.O. Box 1689
Lake Oswego, OR 97035-0889
(503) 620-0222, ext. 320

Fee Arbitration
Fee Arbitration Committee
(Address, telephone same as
   for Attorney Grievance.)

PENNSYLVANIA
Attorney Grievance
State Office:
Chief Disciplinary Counsel
Disciplinary Board of the
   Supreme Court of
   Pennsylvania
300 N. 2nd St.
Harrisburg, PA 17101
(717) 787-1247

Client Security Trust Fund
Executive Director
Pennsylvania Client Security
   Trust Fund
1515 Market St., Suite 1420
Philadelphia, PA 19102
(215) 560-6335

Fee Arbitration
No statewide program;
   disciplinary board refers
   cases to local fee arbitration
   where available.
(Address same as for Attorney
   Grievance.)
(717) 238-6715

PUERTO RICO
Attorney Grievance
Presidente
Comision de Etica Profesional
Colegio de Abogados de
   Puerto Rico
Apartado 1900
San Juan, PR 00903
(809) 721-3358

Secretary
Tribunal Supremo de Puerto
   Rico
Apartado 2392
San Juan, PR 00903
(809) 723-6033

Solicitor General
Departmento de Justicia
Apartado 192
San Juan, PR 00902
(809) 721-2924

Client Security Trust Fund
None.

Fee Arbitration
None.

RHODE ISLAND
Attorney Grievance
State Office:
Chief Disciplinary Counsel
Disciplinary Board of the
   Supreme Court of Rhode
   Island
Supreme Court Bldg.
250 Benefit St., 9th Floor
Providence, RI 02903
(401) 277-3270

Client Security Trust Fund
Executive Director
Rhode Island Bar Association
91 Friendship St.
Providence, RI 02903
(401) 421-5740

Fee Arbitration
Fee Arbitration Committee
(Address, telephone same as
  for Client Security Trust
  Fund.)

SOUTH CAROLINA
Attorney Grievance
State Office:
Administrative Assistant
Board of Commissioners on
  Grievances and Discipline
P.O. Box 11330
Columbia, SC 29211
(803) 734-2038

Client Security Trust Fund
Director of Public Services
South Carolina Bar
950 Taylor St.
P.O. Box 608
Columbia, SC 29202
(803) 799-6653

Fee Arbitration
Resolution of Fee Disputes
  Board
(Address, telephone same as
  for Client Security Trust
  Fund.)

SOUTH DAKOTA
Attorney Grievance
State Office:
Investigator
Disciplinary Board of the State
  Bar of South Dakota
P.O. Box 476
Tyndall, SD 57066
(605) 589-3333

Client Security Trust Fund
Executive Director
State Bar of South Dakota
222 E. Capitol
Pierre, SD 57501
(605) 224-7554

Fee Arbitration
None.

TENNESSEE
Attorney Grievance
State Office:
Chief Disciplinary Counsel
Board of Professional
  Responsibility of the
  Supreme Court of
  Tennessee
1105 Kermit Dr., Suite 730
Nashville, TN 37217
(615) 361-7500

Client Security Trust Fund
Executive Director
Tennessee Bar Association
3622 West End Ave.
Nashville, TN 37205
(615) 383-7421

Fee Arbitration

No statewide program; state
   bar refers cases to local fee
   arbitration where available.
(Address, telephone same as
   for Client Security Trust
   Fund.)

TEXAS
Attorney Grievance

State Office:
General Counsel
State Bar of Texas
P.O. Box 12487
Capitol Station
Austin, TX 78711
(512) 463-1391

Client Security Trust Fund

General Counsel's Office
(Address same as for Attorney
   Grievance.)
(512) 475-6202

Fee Arbitration

No statewide program; state
   bar refers cases to local fee
   arbitration where available.
(Address, telephone same as
   for Attorney Grievance.)

UTAH
Attorney Grievance

State Office:
Bar Counsel
Utah State Bar
645 S. 200 E
Salt Lake City, UT 84111
(801) 531-9110

Client Security Trust Fund

Executive Director
(Address same as for Attorney
   Grievance.)
(801) 531-9077

Fee Arbitration

Fee Arbitration Committee
(Address, telephone same as
   for Attorney Grievance.)

VERMONT
Attorney Grievance

State Office:
Bar Counsel
Supreme Court Building
111 State St.
Montpelier, VT 03602
(802) 828-3204

Client Security Trust Fund

Staff Administrator
Vermont Bar Association
P.O. Box 100
Montpelier, VT 05601
(802) 223-2020

Fee Arbitration

Arbitration of Fee Complaints
   Committee
(Address, telephone same as
   for Client Security Trust
   Fund.)

VIRGINIA
Attorney Grievance

State Office:
Bar Counsel
Virginia State Bar
801 E. Main St., Suite 1000
Richmond, VA 23219
(804) 786-2061

Client Security Trust Fund
Staff Administrator
(Address same as for Attorney
  Grievance.)
(804) 786-2061

Fee Arbitration
No statewide program; state
  bar refers cases to local fee
  arbitration where available.
(Address, telephone same as
  for Attorney Grievance.)

VIRGIN ISLANDS
Attorney Grievance
Chair
Ethics and Grievance
  Committee
U.S. Virgin Islands Bar
  Association
P.O. Box 6520
St. Thomas, VI 00801
(809) 774-6490

Client Security Trust Fund
None.

Fee Arbitration
None.

WASHINGTON
Attorney Grievance
State Office:
Chief Disciplinary Counsel
Washington State Bar
  Association
500 Westin Bldg.
2001 6th Ave.
Seattle, WA 98121-2599
(206) 448-0307

Client Security Trust Fund
General Counsel
(Address, telephone same as
  for Attorney Grievance.)

Fee Arbitration
Fee Arbitration Committee
(Address, telephone same as
  for Attorney Grievance.)

WEST VIRGINIA
Attorney Grievance
State Office:
Bar Counsel
West Virginia State Bar
State Capitol
2006 Kanawha Blvd. E
Charleston, WV 25311
(304) 348-2456

Client Security Trust Fund
Staff Administrator
(Address, telephone same as
  for Attorney Grievance.)

Fee Arbitration
None.

WISCONSIN
Attorney Grievance
State Office:
Administrator
Board of Attorneys
  Professional Responsibility
Supreme Court of Wisconsin
Tenney Bldg.
110 E. Main St., Room 410
Madison, WI 53703
(608) 267-7274

Client Security Trust Fund
Legal Services Assistant
State Bar of Wisconsin
P.O. Box 7158
Madison, WI 53707
(608) 257-3838

Fee Arbitration
Committee on Resolution of
Fee Disputes
(Address, telephone same as
for Client Security Trust
Fund.)

WYOMING

Attorney Grievance
State Office:
Bar Counsel
Wyoming State Bar
P.O. Box 109
Cheyenne, WY 82003-0109
(307) 632-9061

Client Security Trust Fund
Executive Secretary
(Address, telephone same as
for Attorney Grievance.)

Fee Arbitration
Committee on Resolution of
Fee Disputes
(Address, telephone same as
for Attorney Grievance.)

APPENDIX **III**

PROCEDURAL STAGES OF A LAWSUIT

The following flow chart depicts the stages of a typical civil lawsuit. (Criminal lawsuits have different procedures.) This description is general, and because each state and the federal court system has its own procedures, you will have to look at a specific practice-and-procedure book for items such as the names of documents.

Procedural Stages of a Lawsuit: Pleading

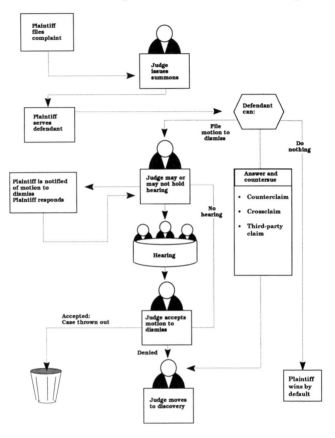

Procedural Stages of a Lawsuit: Discovery

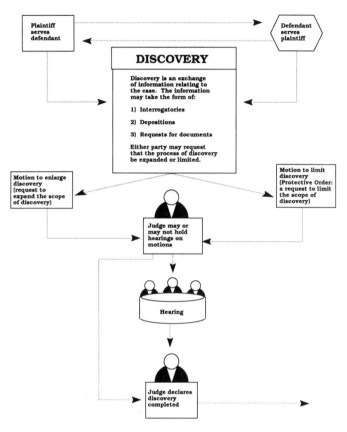

Procedural Stages of a Lawsuit: Pre-Trial

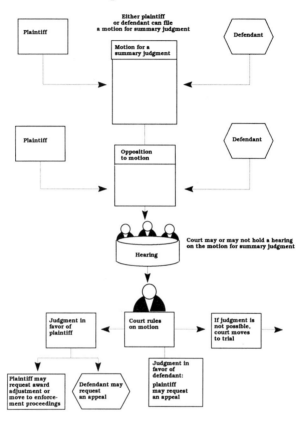

Procedural Stages of a Lawsuit: Trial

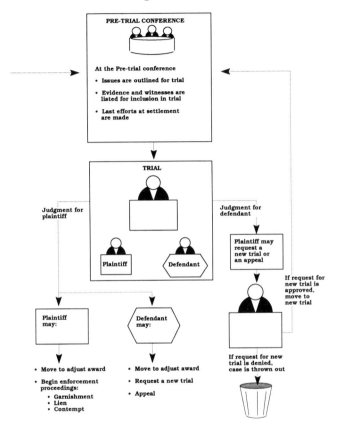

PRIVATE ALTERNATIVE DISPUTE RESOLUTION (ADR) PROGRAMS

The following is a list of private alternative dispute resolution programs. It was compiled, in part, by the American Bar Association's Standing Committee on Dispute Resolution. It is not an exhaustive list. For referrals to other ADR programs, contact one of the national ADR organizations listed or check under "Arbitration" or "Mediation Services" in the telephone Yellow Pages.

NATIONAL ADR ORGANIZATIONS

American Arbitration Association
140 W. 51st St.
New York, NY 10020
(212) 484-2000

Center for Public Resources, Inc.
366 Madison Ave., 14th Floor
New York, NY 10017
(212) 949-6490
(800) 322-6490

Council of Better Business Bureaus (CBBB)
4200 Wilson Blvd., Suite 800
Arlington, VA 22209
(703) 276-0100

Society of Professionals in Dispute Resolution
1730 Rhode Island Ave. NW, Suite 909
Washington, DC 20036
(202) 833-2188

Standing Committee on Dispute Resolution
American Bar Association
1800 M St. NW, Suite 790
Washington, DC 20036
(202) 331-2258

LOCAL ADR ORGANIZATIONS

ALASKA

Peninsula Mediation
Sara L. Jackinsky
P.O. Box 1044
Homer, AK 99603-1044
(907) 235-6417

ARIZONA

U.S. Arbitration &
    Mediation/Arizona
Brice Buehler
7226 N. 16th St., Suite 200
Phoenix, AZ 85020
(602) 870-4400

CALIFORNIA

ADRA
Nancy Yeend
399 Sherman Ave., Suite 5
Palo Alto, CA 94306
(415) 328-2372

American Intermediation
    Service
114 Sansome St., Suite 1130
San Francisco, CA 94104
(415) 788-6253

Judicial Arbitration &
    Mediation Service, Inc.
111 Pine St., Suite 205
San Francisco, CA 94111-5609
(415) 982-5267

Mediation Law Offices
Gary Friedman
34 Forrest St.
Mill Valley, CA 94941
(415) 383-1300

Northern California Mediation
    Center
Deborah Mathews
100 Tamal Plaza, Suite 175
Corte Madera, CA 94925
(415) 927-1422

COLORADO

Arnold Swartz & Associates
Arnold Swartz
720 Kipling St., Suite 200
Lakewood, CO 80215
(303) 237-4828

CONNECTICUT

Dispute Resolution, Inc.
Michael Lockaby
179 Allyn St., Suite 508
Hartford, CT 06103
(203) 724-0861

DISTRICT OF COLUMBIA

Negotiated Solutions
Larry Kahn
1900 L St. NW, Suite 500
Washington, DC 20036
(202) 785-5800

FLORIDA

Florida Mediation Group
Allene Nicholson
P.O. Box 864
South Beach, FL 33119-0864
(305) 532-2933

HAWAII

Pacific Arbitration &
 Mediation Services
Bradley A. Coates
900 Fort St. Mall, Suite 1400
Honolulu, HI 96813
(808) 524-4854

IDAHO

Idaho Arbitration Services
Ed Litteneker
P.O. Box 321
322 Main St.
Lewiston, ID 83501-0321
(208) 746-0806

ILLINOIS

Resolve Dispute Management,
 Inc.
Brian Muldoon
650 N. Dearborn, 4th Floor
Chicago, IL 60610
(312) 943-7477

INDIANA

U.S. Arbitration/Indiana
Jeffrey Abbott
2345 S. Lynhurst Dr., Suite 213
Indianapolis, IN 46241
(317) 243-2174

LOUISIANA

U.S. Arbitration &
 Mediation/Gulf South
Eldon Harvey
3748 N. Causeway Blvd.,
 Suite 201
Metairie, LA 70002
(504) 831-2141

MARYLAND

U.S. Arbitration &
 Mediation/Northeast
Virginia Deardorff
9515 Deereco Rd., Suite 500
Timonium, MD 21093
(301) 252-0395

MASSACHUSETTS

ENDISPUTE, Inc.
Mike Fields
955 Massachusetts Ave., 7th
 Floor
Cambridge, MA 02139
(617) 868-0200

MICHIGAN

Ann Arbor Mediation Center
Zena D. Zumeta
330 E. Liberty, Suite 3-A
Ann Arbor, MI 48104
(313) 663-1155

MINNESOTA

EQUILAW, Inc.
Stephen P. Doyle
2124 Dupont Ave. S
Minneapolis, MN 55405
(612) 871-9205

U.S. Arbitration &
 Mediation/Minnesota
Kim McCandless
8400 Normandale Lake Blvd.,
 Suite 909
Minneapolis, MN 55437
(612) 893-9584

MISSOURI

Midwest Arbitration &
   Mediation
Richard Routman
P.O. Box 26064
Kansas City, MO 64196-6064
(816) 221-4079

U.S. Arbitration &
   Mediation/Midwest
Robert Crowe
915 Olive St., Suite 1001C
St. Louis, MO 63101
(314) 231-4642

MONTANA

Settlement Solutions
Roy H. Andes
210 N. Higgins Ave.
Missoula, MT 59802
(406) 728-7295

NEBRASKA

U.S. Arbitration/Nebraska
Frederick S. Cassman
8712 W. Dodge Rd., Suite 300
Omaha, NE 68114
(402) 392-1250

NEW JERSEY

ADR Center
Ron Kubiak
P.O. Box 252
Collingswood, NJ 08108-0252
(609) 869-0400

NEW MEXICO

U.S. Arbitration &
   Mediation/New Mexico
Brice Buehler
365 Alda Rd. SW
Rio Rancho, NM 87124
(800) 235-3746

NEW YORK

ENDISPUTE, Inc.
Michael Young
461 Park Ave. S, Suite 600
New York, NY 10016
(212) 725-6160

NORTH CAROLINA

Private Adjudication Center
Rene Stemple Ellis
3101 Petty Rd., Suite 207
Durham, NC 27707
(919) 493-7770

OHIO

U.S. Arbitration &
   Mediation/Ohio
William L. Clark
1580 Fishinger Rd.
Columbus, OH 43221
(614) 459-1012

OKLAHOMA

Oklahoma Mediation/
   Arbitration Service
John Rothman
7666 E. 61st St., Suite 335
Tulsa, OK 74133
(918) 459-0100

OREGON

Judicial Arbitration &
   Mediation Service, Inc.
1001 S.W. 5th Ave., Suite 1000
Portland, OR 97204
(503) 224-1210

PENNSYLVANIA

American Intermediation
   Service
Dennis K. Heir
Ten Penn Center, Suite 1000
Philadelphia, PA 19103
(800) 826-5605

U.S. Arbitration &
   Mediation/Northeast
1424 Chestnut St.
Philadelphia, PA 19102
(215) 750-6970

TEXAS

Judicial Arbitration &
   Mediation Service, Inc.
3102 Oak Lawn, Suite 700
Dallas, TX 75219
(214) 744-5267

Mediation Services, Inc.
Gary J. Kirkpatrick
3503 Fairmont at Turtle Creek
Dallas, TX 75219-4704
(214) 526-1044

U.S. Arbitration &
   Mediation/Southwest
Lila Abrams
12700 Hillcrest Rd., Suite 211
Dallas, TX 75230
(214) 490-6394

VIRGINIA

David W. Mullen
111 E. Roanoke St.
Christinsburg, VA 24073
(703) 382-8296

Tazewell T. Hubard, III
125 St. Paul's Blvd.
Norfolk, VA 23510
(804) 627-6120

WASHINGTON

David Skeen
1535 Jefferson St.
Port Townsend, WA 98368
(206) 385-1544

Northwest Mediation Service
Tena Crosby
405 114th Ave. SE, Suite 300
Bellevue, WA 98004
(206) 455-3989

U.S. Arbitration & Mediation,
   Inc.
Michael S. Gillie
83 S. King St., Suite 806
Seattle, WA 98104
(206) 467-0793

WISCONSIN

Howard S. Bellman
119 Martin Luther King Blvd.,
   Suite 413
Madison, WI 53703
(608) 255-9393

WYOMING

U.S. Arbitration/Wyoming
Les Bowron
137 N. Beech St.
Casper, WY 82601
(307) 237-1983

GLOSSARY
OF TERMS

The following terms are used in this book or in litigation generally. Italicized terms in definitions are themselves defined in other entries.

Admonition   See *Reprimand.*

Affidavit   Written statement of fact voluntarily signed and sworn to before a person who has authority to administer an oath; it can be used in court as *evidence.*

Answer   *Defendant*'s formal written statement of defense against the *plaintiff*'s complaint in a lawsuit. The answer addresses the truth or falsity of the plaintiff's claims and can include a *counterclaim.*

Appeal   Request that a higher court review the decision of a lower court to correct errors in the application of law or procedure.

Appellant   Person who initiates an *appeal.*

Arbitration   Method of settling disputes in which the two sides submit arguments to a neutral third party or panel, which makes a decision after listening to both sides and considering the evidence.

Attorney discipline   Act by a state bar grievance committee or court sanctioning a lawyer for violating the state's *rules of professional conduct.*

Breach of contract   Reason for suing based on failure to live up to a legally binding promise, such as the terms of a client-attorney agreement.

Brief   Written statement prepared by one side in a lawsuit to explain to a judge the essential facts of a case and the applicable law.

Censure   See *Reprimand.*

Client security trust fund   State bar program in which money collected from attorneys is used to reimburse victims of lawyer theft.

Comingling   Lawyer misuse of a client's funds by mingling them with the lawyer's personal money. This is a violation of every state's *rules of professional conduct.*

Common law   Law derived by U.S. courts from early English court decisions, not from legislative enactment or constitutional provisions.

Complaint   Document that officially initiates a lawsuit. It includes, among other things, a statement of the facts and allegation of the wrong or harm done to the one making the complaint *(plaintiff)* by the other side *(defendant);* a request for help from the court; and an explanation of why the court has the power to comply with that request.

Conflict of interest   Attorney's association or tie that would jeopardize or bias representation of the client. Failing to disclose a potential conflict of interest to a client is a violation of every state's *rules of professional conduct.*

Contempt   Willful disobedience of a judge's command or an official court order, punishable by fine or imprisonment.

Contingency fee   Attorney's fee based on a percentage of the amount awarded to the client. If no amount is awarded, no fee must be paid, although the client will be required to pay legal *expenses.*

Continuance   Postponement of a legal proceeding.

Counter-claim   Claim made by a *defendant* in a civil lawsuit that, in effect, sues the *plaintiff.*

Damages   Amount of money or other relief requested by the *plaintiff* in a lawsuit.

Default judgment   Decision in favor of the *plaintiff* because the *defendant* failed to file a response to the plaintiff's complaint within the time required by law, or failed to appear in court on the scheduled date of the hearing or trial.

Defendant   Person against whom a legal action is filed.

Deposition   Out-of-court process of taking the sworn testimony of a witness. This is usually done by a lawyer with a lawyer from the other side being permitted to attend or participate. The purpose is to disclose relevant information so that each side can evaluate its case before going to trial and decide whether to pursue the claim or settle out of court.

Disbarment   Removing a lawyer's license to practice in a state for violating that state's *rules of professional conduct.* This is the most severe form of *attorney discipline.* In most states a lawyer may reapply for admission to practice five years after being disbarred.

Disciplinary agency   State agency that processes *complaints* against lawyers to determine if the *rules of professional conduct* have been violated sufficiently to warrant *attorney discipline.* Also called *grievance committee.*

Discovery   Before-trial formal and informal exchange of information between the sides in a lawsuit. Two types of discovery are *interrogatories* and *depositions.*

Discovery rule   One of three possible rules states may use to set a deadline or *statute of limitations* for filing a malpractice lawsuit. States that use the discovery rule hold that the statute of limitations "clock" does not begin to run until the client knows or should know that the injury has occurred.

Economic loss   Damages a *plaintiff* can demonstrate with bills, receipts or other financial statements.

Evidence   Any type of information (documents, concrete items, observations, etc.) presented at trial that either reinforces or contests a disputed matter's validity.

Expenses   Charges for a lawyer's work other than fees, typically including long-distance telephone charges, photocopying, court filing fees and expert witness fees.

Fee arbitration   Out-of-court forum for settling fee disputes between attorneys and clients. Many state and local bar associations have established fee arbitration committees.

Flat fee   Lawyer's fee based on a fixed amount for handling a legal matter regardless of the time spent or the difficulty of the tasks involved. Legal clinics and some lawyers charge flat rates for routine, uncontested matters such as name changes, simple wills and uncontested divorces.

Good cause   If a client fires an attorney for good cause, as defined by the state bar, the client may not be legally required to pay for all the attorney's services.

Grievance committee   See *Disciplinary agency.*

Hourly fee   Lawyer's fee based on the amount of time worked on a case. The fee is the hourly rate multiplied by the number of hours worked.

In pro per   See *Pro se.*

Interrogatory   Form of *discovery* in which written questions posed by one side in a lawsuit require written responses under oath by the other.

Judgment   Final decision announced or written by a judge about the rights and claims of each side in a lawsuit.

Legal malpractice   Misconduct that, in the course of handling a case, harms a client. Most legal malpractice lawsuits are based on claims of *negligence* or *breach of contract.*

Mediation   Informal alternative to suing in which both sides to a dispute meet with a neutral third party (mediator) to negotiate a resolution. The resolution is usually put into a written agreement that is signed by both sides.

Motion   Request that a judge take specific action. (Example: a "motion to dismiss" is a request that the judge throw a case out of court.)

Negligence   Legal doctrine on which a lawsuit is based, whereby the person being sued is accused of failing to do something that would normally be expected. Many *legal malpractice* cases are based on negligence.

Order   Written command by a judge or court clerk describing a decision of the court, directing or forbidding an action, or issuing the final ruling of the court in a case.

Plaintiff   Person who files a lawsuit against another.

Pleading   Making a formal written statement of the claims or defenses of each side in a lawsuit.

Pretrial conference   Meeting of the lawyers and the judge, sometimes also including the parties to a lawsuit, to narrow the issues in the lawsuit, to agree on what will be presented at the trial and to make a final effort to settle the case without trial.

Pro se   Representing yourself in court without the help of an attorney. Also called *in pro per.*

Proximate causation   The direct connection between an event and the result that proves fault. In a *legal malpractice* case, the client must show that the attorney's misconduct or *negligence* was the "proximate cause" of the loss in order to recover money.

Reprimand   *Attorney discipline* whereby an attorney is either privately or publicly chastised for violating the state's *rules of professional conduct.* In both instances the lawyer is sent a letter explaining the misconduct and discipline. Also called a *censure* or *admonition.*

Respondent   (1) The person against whom a *motion* is filed. (2) The person against whom an *appeal* is taken.

Retainer   Money asked by the lawyer before beginning work on a case, often considered a deposit for a portion of the work to be done. The money may be used to cover *expenses* or the lawyer's fee or simply to reserve the lawyer's services for a specified time period or a lawsuit. The unused portion may or may not be refundable.

Rules of professional conduct Rules that govern a lawyer's right to practice law in a state. A lawyer's license can be removed or suspended, or the lawyer can be reprimanded, for violating the code. Each state's code is based on the American Bar Association's model code.

Ruling A judge's decision on a legal question raised during a lawsuit.

Service The delivery of a legal document by an officially authorized person to meet formal requirements of the applicable laws and assure that the person being sued is formally notified about the lawsuit or other legal action.

Settlement An agreement about the final disposition of a lawsuit, including payment of debts, costs and so forth.

Statute of limitations A law that sets a time deadline for filing a lawsuit. This varies from state to state and with the basis of the lawsuit.

Subpoena A court notice to compel the appearance of a witness or submission of documents or other evidence at a hearing; disobedience may be punishable as contempt of court.

Summons (1) A notice delivered by a sheriff or other authorized person informing a *defendant* about a lawsuit. It notifies the defendant to appear in court at a specified time to respond to allegations in the lawsuit or risk losing the suit because of absence *(default judgment)*. (2) A notice delivered by a sheriff or other authorized person informing someone to appear before a grand jury.

Summary judgment A court's final decision based on the facts but issued before the end of a full trial.

Suspension Discipline removing a lawyer's license to practice law in a specific state for a period of time ranging from a few days to several years for violating the *rules of professional conduct.*

Testimony Oral or written evidence in the form of questions and answers given under oath.

Tort A private wrong that causes injury to a person or property. Some *legal malpractice* cases are tort cases.

Withdrawal An attorney's decision to stop working on a case and notification of the client about that decision.

BIBLIOGRAPHY

The following list includes books that deal with: hiring and managing lawyers; legal malpractice; and national directories of attorneys' names and addresses. The legal malpractice section includes the resources HALT relied on most in its research, but it is by no means an exhaustive list of what's available on legal malpractice. For that, check a law library or your public library's index. The books listed as out of print are available only in libraries.

Client-Attorney Relations

Competent Counsel: Working with Lawyers, by Denise G. Shekerjian. Dodd, Mead & Co., 6 Ram Ridge Rd., Spring Valley, NY 10977. 1985. $15.95. 187 pages. (Out of print.)
   Advice on shopping for and managing a lawyer, legal costs, attorney discipline and legal malpractice cases. Also includes advice about alternatives to hiring a lawyer and a complete list of state grievance committees.

Kill All the Lawyers? A Client's Guide to Hiring, Firing, Using and Suing Lawyers, by Sloan Bashinsky. Prentice-Hall, Gulf and Western Plaza, New York, NY 10023. 1986. $12.95. 148 pages.
   Anecdotes about lawyers, judges and clients. In sections with titles like "Greedy Lawyers," "Fee Generators" and "Clients Who Don't Pay," Bashinsky gives advice on what it is clients expect from lawyers, whether they can get it and at what cost.

The Lawyer Book: A Nuts and Bolts Guide to Client Survival, by Wesley J. Smith. Price/Stern/Sloan Publishers, 360 N. La Cienega Blvd., Los Angeles, CA 90048. 1987. $9.95. 239 pages.

In large print with many illustrations. Shopping, managing and problem-solving techniques for maintaining a healthy client-attorney relationship. Includes information about fee setting and suggests what legal tasks you can and cannot do on your own. Introduction by Ralph Nader.

One Hundred Ways to Cut Legal Fees & Manage Your Lawyer, by Erwin G. Krasnow and Robin S. Conrad. National Chamber Litigation Center, 1615 H St. NW, Washington, DC 20006. 1988. $10.95. 143 pages.

Useful guide that presents lawyers as business people who need responsible, active management by their clients. Contains a bibliography and a list of federal statutes that authorize recovering attorneys' fees under certain circumstances.

Putting a Lid on Legal Fees: How to Deal Effectively with Lawyers, by Raymond M. Klein. Interlink Press, 908 Kenfield Ave., Los Angeles, CA 90049. 1986. $12.95. 189 pages.

Intended for business clients; includes advice and information that is useful for other clients as well. The basic advice: "Participate, don't abdicate." Covers shopping for, hiring and managing a lawyer, with special emphasis on how fees are generated, what litigation can cost and how to keep down legal fees.

The Terrible Truth about Lawyers: How Lawyers Really Work & How to Deal with Them Successfully, by Mark H. McCormack. Beech Tree Books, William Morrow & Co., 105 Madison Ave., New York, NY 10016. 1987. $17.95. 260 pages.

Written for business clients. Draws on the author's personal experience as both a lawyer and a business client to educate about client-attorney relations. Uses anecdotes to illustrate points and axioms. Example: attorney fees are discussed under the axiom, "They'll spend more of it, the less the client seems to care."

Using a Lawyer—And What to Do If Things Go Wrong, by Kay Ostberg in Association with HALT. A Random House Practical Law Manual, Random House, 201 E. 50th St., New York, NY 10022. 1990. $8.95. 146 pages.

Complete self-help guide to shopping for, managing and working with a lawyer. Also includes fee negotiation strategies, a state-by-state list of lawyer grievance committees and sample fee agreements.

What Every Client Needs to Know about Using a Lawyer, by Gregory White Smith & Steven Naifeh. G. P. Putnam's Sons, 200 Madison Ave., New York, NY 10016. 1982. $13.95. 240 pages. (Out of print.)

Comprehensive "how-to" book by two Harvard Law School graduates. Addresses clients' biggest fears—that lawyers are too expensive, dishonest or incompetent. To prevent those fears from becoming realities, offers advice on shopping for, managing and paying lawyers. Also includes a good discussion of legal malpractice.

What Lawyers Do . . . And How to Make Them Work for You, by Daniel R. White, E. P. Dutton, 2 Park Ave., New York, NY 10016. 1987. $17.95. 306 pages. (Out of print.)

Describes the use and role of lawyers in some of the most common legal situations people face, such as family law, taxes, estate planning, housing and death. Usually advises hiring a lawyer, but does list alternatives such as mediation and legal clinics.

What You Aren't Supposed to Know about the Legal Profession—An Exposé of Lawyers, Law Schools, Judges and More, by Laurens R. Schwartz. Shapolsky Publishers, 136 W. 22nd St., New York, NY 10011. 1988. $14.95. 173 pages.

Inside, humorous glimpse at why lawyers think and behave the way they do. Sometimes irreverent, always funny and revealing, Schwartz pokes fun at law school training, law firm antics and the legal profession in general. Does not include systematic advice on hiring or working with attorneys.

Winning with Your Lawyer: What Every Client Should Know about How the Legal System Works, by Burton Marks and Gerald Goldfarb. McGraw-Hill, 1221 Ave. of the Americas, New York, NY 10021. 1987 (2nd Ed.). $8.00. 242 pages. (Out of print.)

The first part offers tips on selecting and working with attorneys; the second on how to manage attorneys in specific legal situations (personal injury, divorce, estate planning, crime and property rights).

Legal Malpractice Resources

American Jurisprudence, Second Edition, Vol. 7 (*Am. Jur.* 2d) The Lawyers Cooperative Publishing Co., Aqueduct Bldg., Rochester, NY 14694. 1980. See especially: "Liability of Attorneys for Malpractice," Sections 197–231. Available at law libraries.

Legal encyclopedia of general information about various types of law and legal concepts. Written in plain English. Includes cross-references and bibliographies to direct the reader to primary sources.

Corpus Juris Secundum, Vol. 7A (*C.J.S.*). West Publishing Co., 50 W. Kellogg Blvd., St. Paul, MN 55164. 1980. See especially: "Liability for Negligence or Malpractice," Sections 255–276.

More comprehensive legal encyclopedia series than *Am. Jur.* but written only for lawyers and harder to understand. General information about various types of law and legal concepts. Includes case law citations.

How to Sue Your Lawyer: The Consumer Guide to Legal Malpractice, by Hilton L. Stein. Legal Malpractice Institute, 103 Washington St., Morristown, NJ 07960. 1989. $19.95. 266 pages.

Step-by-step guide for filing a legal malpractice case. The author calls on personal experience to detail what goes on in a typical malpractice case.

Lawyers' Manual on Professional Conduct. American Bar Association and Bureau of National Affairs, 1231 25th St. NW, Washington, DC 20037. 1984. See especially: Legal Malpractice, Section 301, pages 101–901. Available at library.

In plain English and for lawyers, a 2,000-plus-page looseleaf book intended for lawyers who handle malpractice cases. Includes practical information on a wide variety of topics, including legal malpractice, the full text of the ABA Model Rules of Professional Conduct and selected ABA ethics opinions from state and local bar associations.

Legal Malpractice, by Ronald E. Mallen and Jeffrey M. Smith. West Publishing Co., 50 W. Kellogg Blvd., St. Paul, MN 55164. 2 volumes. 1989 (3rd Ed.). $137.80. 1,965 pages.

In plain English, but intended for lawyers. The most comprehensive resource available on laws governing legal malpractice litigation. Includes an exhaustive list of cases. To avoid investing the purchase price, try to find it in a public library or local law library.

Modern Legal Ethics, by Charles W. Wolfram. West Publishing Co., 50 W. Kellogg Blvd., St. Paul, MN 55164. 1986 (1st Ed.). $28.95. 1,114 pages.

Broad, in-depth analysis of a lawyer's responsibilities, written for law students. Theoretical summary of current law and discussion of possible future trends. Also summarizes current malpractice cases and related topics. Discusses lawyer and legal system regulation, professional discipline, the client-attorney relationship, competence, etc.

Professional Negligence Law Reporter. Association of Trial Lawyers of America, Education Fund, 1050 31st St. NW, Washington, DC 20007-4499. Published monthly. $195.

Short and accurate summaries of the facts, parties and awards given in professional negligence cases. Lists cases from all types of professions including legal, medical and accounting. Also lists who plaintiff's counsel was.

Profile of Legal Malpractice: A Statistical Study of Determinative Characteristics of Claims Asserted Against Attorneys. Standing Committee on Lawyers' Professional Liability, American Bar Association, 750 N. Lake Shore Dr., Chicago, IL 60611. 1986. Free. 81 pages.

Statistical analysis of 29,227 malpractice claims against attorneys between 1983 and 1985. Graphs and charts present data about the nature and size of legal malpractice complaints. (For example, the types of errors that yield the most complaints.)

Lawyer Shopping Directories

The American Lawyer Guide to Leading Law Firms, by Steven Brill. AM-Law Publishing Co., New York, NY 10016. 2 volumes. 1983–1984. 2,029 pages. (Out of print.)

An alphabetical list of 234 law firms by city. Each firm's entry is extensive, including the percentage of lawyers in the firm by specialty, names of some clients and the law school most of its attorneys attended. The lawyers and firms listed work in almost every area of law *except* malpractice law.

The Best Lawyers in America, by Steven Naifeh and Gregory White Smith. Putnam Publishing Group, 20 Madison Ave., New York, NY 10016. 1984. 240 pages. (Out of print.)

Almost 200 lawyers listed by specialty, such as domestic relations, trusts and estates, criminal defense, creditors' and debtors' rights and civil litigation. No biographical information. The lawyers were selected based on questionnaires completed by 2,000 lawyers.

Directory of the Legal Profession, by Ben Gerson. N.Y. Law Publishing Co., New York, NY 10016. 1984. 1,111 pages. (Out of print.)

More than 600 firms listed alphabetically by state and city. The entries include listing by specialty such as litigation, labor, general business, corporate, real estate and entertainment/sports.

Law & Business Directory of Litigation Attorneys, by Prentice-Hall Law & Business in cooperation with the American Bar Association Section of Litigation, 270 Sylvan Ave., Englewood Cliffs, NJ 07632. 2 volumes. 1990. $350. 6,800 pages.

Lists 31,000 litigators alphabetically by state and city. Each entry includes biography, with lawyer's name, address, firm, specialization, significant cases and education. The directory identifies 90 different areas in which litigators might specialize.

Lawyer Directory. District of Columbia Bar, 1707 L Street NW, 6th Floor, Washington, DC 20036. 1990 (11th Ed.). $10. 144 pages.

Washington, D.C., lawyers listed alphabetically by specialty. Short biography on each lawyer includes firm, address, fee information and education.

Lawyers' Register by Specialties and Fields of Law, by Margaret A. Schultz. Lawyers' Register Publishing Company, 30700 Bainbridge Rd., Suite H, Solon, OH 44139. 1988 (9th Ed.). $99.50. 801 pages.

About 1,000 lawyers by specialties, such as municipal law, negligence and medical/legal malpractice. Each entry includes the lawyer's name, address, specialization and, in some cases, a biographical note supplied by the lawyer. Lawyers are those suggested by the ABA.

Martindale-Hubbell Law Directory. Martindale-Hubbell, 630 Central Ave., New Providence, NJ 07974. 8 volumes. 1988. $195.

600,000 American and Canadian lawyers, listed alphabetically by state and by categories (U.S. government, international, patent lawyers). Each entry has an extensive biography, including the lawyer's education, specialty, law firm, date of admittance to the bar and a "rating." This rating is of little practical value, however, as it is based on information supplied by fellow lawyers—not by clients.

Who's Who in American Law. Macmillan Directory Division, 3002 Glenview Rd., Wilmette, IL 60091. 1987–88 (5th Ed.). Approximately $165. 974 pages.

About 24,000 lawyers listed alphabetically. Finding a lawyer in a specific state or with a specific expertise requires browsing through the entire directory. Includes biographical notes on each lawyer. The publisher selected lawyers by assessing "incumbency in a defined position of responsibility" or "attainment of a significant level of achievement."

APPENDIX VII

ADDING NAMES TO
THE DIRECTORY

Send us your recommendations. If you've had a good working relationship with a particular legal malpractice attorney, send his or her name, address and telephone number to HALT using the form below. (A photocopy will do.) We will invite the lawyer to complete a questionnaire about practice policies (fees, negotiations, written agreements, etc.) and, based on the answers received, to participate in our attorney referral network.

We may also update this directory during the coming years. If you have a name to add or more recent information about one of the attorneys listed, please let us know. Although we can't promise to include all the names sent in, we do appreciate your recommendations.

Name: _____

Street: _____

City: _____ State _____ Zip _____

Telephone: __(_____)_____

Send to:

HALT
1319 F Street N.W., Suite 300
Washington, D.C. 20004

About the Author

Kay Ostberg is the Deputy Director of HALT. She is the author of *Using a Lawyer, Probate, Everyday Contracts* and the "Attorney Discipline National Survey and Report." Ms. Ostberg received her J.D. in 1983 from the National Law Center at George Washington University. She is a member of the National Federation of Paralegal Associations Advisory Board.